You Did
It for Me

You Did It for Me

Care of Your Neighbor as a Spiritual Practice

Kevin E. McKenna

ave maria press A̲m̲p̲ **Notre Dame, Indiana**

International Standard Book Number: 1-59471-039-2

Cover and text design by Andrew Borys

Printed and bound in the United States of America.

Library of Congress Cataloging-in-Publication Data

McKenna, Kevin E., 1950-
  You did it for me : care of your neighbor as a spiritual practice / Kevin E. McKenna.
       p. cm.
  Includes bibliographical references.
  ISBN 1-59471-039-2 (pbk.)
  1. Christian sociology--Catholic Church. 2. Christian life--Catholic authors. 3. Catholic Church--Doctrines. I. Title.

BX1753.M233 2005
261.8'088'282--dc22

                                   2004026503

To the community of Saint Cecilia Parish, Rochester, New York, in appreciation for their wisdom, patience and support, as they teach me each day about "living the gospel."

Contents

Introduction

One of the great secrets of the Catholic church has been its Catholic social teaching. This tradition is found essentially in the collection of encyclicals on social justice issued by several popes beginning with Pope Leo XIII in 1891 in the historic *Rerum Novarum*. Although the doctrinal beliefs of the Catholic church and its confessional faith are well known, the teachings about social justice are not as well known or even understood.

This body of teachings has many scriptural sources—for example, the prophets found in Hebrew Scripture who proclaimed God's special love for the poor and the oppressed and invited the people of Israel to a special covenant of justice and love with Yahweh their God. Prophets such as Amos, the shepherd of Tekoa in Judah, railed against the hollow prosperity during the reign of Jeroboam II, summoning the people to their true religious and moral foundations in God's law.

> Seek good and not evil,
>   that you may live;
> Then truly will the LORD, the God of hosts,
>   be with you as you claim!
> Hate evil and love good,
>   and let justice prevail at the gate;
> Then it may be that the LORD, the God of
>   hosts,
>   will have pity on the remnant of Joseph.
>   (Am 5:14–15)

Catholic social teaching is strongly rooted in the life and teachings of Jesus Christ, who proclaimed a gospel of love, justice, and a special concern for the poor, the hungry stranger and the outcast.

> "Then the just will ask him: 'Lord, when did we see you hungry and feed you or see you thirsty and give you drink? When did we welcome you away from home or clothe you in your nakedness? When did we visit you when you were ill or in prison?' The king will answer them: 'I assure you, as often as you did it for one of my least brothers, you did it for me.'"
>
> (Mt 25:37–40)

In addition to Leo XIII's *Rerum Novarum* that addressed the plight of the nineteenth-century worker in Christian terms, several popes have issued encyclicals, attempting to make scriptural teachings applicable to modern day humanity's moral struggles and issues. Likewise, bishops' conferences such as that in the United States, the United States Conference of Catholic Bishops (U.S.C.C.B), formerly the National Conference of Catholic Bishops (N.C.C.B.) and United States Catholic Conference (U.S.C.C.) have attempted to make meaningful application of the mandate of Jesus Christ to love God and our neighbor. Through the years these conferences have issued various statements and pastoral letters, calling Christians to an active demonstration of Christian faith. The aim has been to reiterate the interrelation of the social teachings of the church and daily life: "Catholic social teaching is based on and inseparable from our understanding of human life and human dignity. Every human being is created in the image of God and redeemed by Jesus Christ and therefore is invaluable and worthy of respect as a member of the human family."[1]

Jesus himself pressed home the need for concrete actions on behalf of those in need as an essential element of the Kingdom. In Chapter 10 of Luke's gospel Jesus shares the parable of "the Good Samaritan," in response to the inquiry of a lawyer who questions him, "Who is my neighbor?" The expansive definition of charity illustrated by this parable—the Samaritan, enemy of the Jews is the only one to come to the aid of the victim left wounded on the highway—discloses the universal thrust of compassion to be shown by Jesus' followers to others in need. Thomas Merton succinctly summarizes the gospel injunction of concern for neighbor in both its dimensions: alleviating needs and working to alleviate the causes for injustice that at times result in the original need. "Christian charity is no longer real unless it is accompanied by a concern for social justice."[2]

The Good News of Jesus presents a path of life often quite different from the way of the world. "The gospel is the most counter-cultural and the most significantly revolutionary document one could ever hope to find. It reveals the meaning and purpose of human life in terms which are close to being absolutely contradictory to the form of perceiving and valuing human persons in our culture."[3] The way of the gospel points to a narrow path that leads to life lived to its fullness. With baptism, the Christian begins a lifetime of conversion, living in the world but not being mastered by it, following the "way of the Teacher" and inviting fellow pilgrims to seek the truth. "The world needs people who seek truth, the ultimate meaning of life—saving truth. It needs people who pursue it in an honest exchange of genuine convictions in discussion with others."[4] Christians rejoice in finding the truth in Jesus and his teachings.

Saint Paul was one of the earliest of those who left all to follow the teachings of the itinerant carpenter-preacher. So convinced was he of the truth of the message and its potential for giving new life that he traveled throughout the known world preaching the message of Jesus Christ. Paul's letter to the Galatians recounts his conversion experience to a new way of life, in which he became Christ-centered in all things. He would henceforth live his life centered on his relationship with Jesus Christ, the one "who loved me, and gave himself for me" (Gal 2:20). His well-known valedictory to the power of love (1 Cor 13) shows the concern that a relationship with Jesus flows forth into practical implementation.

In less dramatic ways perhaps but with nonetheless similar conviction, each Christian is called to live the gospel of Jesus Christ. The social teachings of the church give clear guidance and practical ways to live "the Message." For example, many of the social justice encyclicals contain scriptural warrants given by Christ ("as often as you did it for the least of my brethren, you did it to me"), combined with an analysis of a particular contemporary problem, concluding with concrete applications. Thus important directives by Jesus to love God and neighbor are seen to have urgent practical consequences today. "All people of good will can learn, from those who are guided by the Spirit of God, that they cannot dwell in the truth unless they effectively take sides with the unloved, the oppressed, the downtrodden."[5] The Congregation for the Doctrine of the Faith in 1986 in its *Instruction on Christian Freedom and Liberation*, provided a helpful context to understand the role of the church's social justice tradition: "The Church's social teaching is born of the encounter of the gospel message and of its demands summarized in the supreme commandment of love of God and neighbor in justice with the problems emanating from the life of society."[6]

The teachings in this area continue to grow dynamically, as the church faces more and more complex moral issues. As we shall see, the basis of the teachings has not changed, but the church has a constant need to update and refine the language and concepts used to teach timeless truths. "Hence, the Church periodically improves upon the language used in its teaching to deepen its knowledge of the truth it possesses."[7] The church must continually evaluate the circumstances in which she finds herself, the needs presented to her at any particular time and then, after much study, set forth the appropriate teaching in a clear, understandable manner. In this way, a continuous and consistent message is proclaimed concerning principles of gospel justice, adapted to the new problems and situations in the world which need clarification from a faith perspective.

The way of leading a Christian life is certainly not *limited* to knowing and following the "social gospel" of the church. Rather, it is an integration of many components. Doing works of justice should not be separated from a vital and personal relationship with Jesus Christ. "Tithing one's time for the marginal, for it to be an authentic and lasting commitment, can be maintained only by a life of prayer, community life, and the intimacy of centering and resting in the truth of prayer."[8] But neither should a life of prayer be immune or separated from concrete, practical efforts at living the teachings that Jesus proclaimed.

The U.S. Catholic bishops have summarized the social teachings of the church in terms of seven broad themes:

- Respect for the life and dignity of each person

- Call to Family, Community, and Participation

- Rights and Responsibilities of the Human Person

- Option for and With the Poor and Vulnerable

- Dignity of Work and the Rights of Workers

- Solidarity

- Care for God's Creation

These themes provide a helpful outline for viewing the social teachings that have developed over these last one hundred years. I believe that, with careful and prayerful study, they present a way of life for the Christian who seeks to live the gospel of Jesus Christ today, since the themes direct us in specific ways to make contemporary the mission and message of Jesus Christ. I have taken the liberty of altering the order in which the themes are normally presented, beginning with "Care for God's Creation." I believe that one of the hallmarks of Catholic identity has been our understanding of God's presence in the world from which can develop our appreciation of his presence in our neighbor, the community, etc.

I present these themes for reflection as a fellow pilgrim and accept them as a challenge to my own spiritual growth and development, realizing that I have many miles to go in my own journey as a disciple of the Lord Jesus.

This book therefore evolves from the seven specific themes of social teaching and provides in each chapter an "extended meditation" on one of the themes. It relies heavily on the teachings of the popes and bishops and summaries of pertinent church documents on social teaching and includes many of the original documents' recommendations on living the gospel today effectively. I have found my own approach to spirituality to be developing by reflecting on these church documents not as an academic exercise but rather as a means of meditating on how I might better live the teachings of Jesus in a practical way. While preparing the manuscript for an earlier work, *A Concise Guide to Catholic Social Teaching*, I found myself deeply affected while reading Pope John Paul II's *Evangelium Vitae, The Gospel of Life*, his extended treatise on the dignity of the human person and today's modern challenges to this value, especially for those in the womb. I began to realize gradually how well this and other similar teachings integrates in a concrete way the demands of the gospel for justice and respect for all God's creatures from a very personal starting point: our own creation by a loving and personal God. It is my hope that the reader will be stimulated to read the original document from which quotations and summaries are extracted. Reflection questions conclude each chapter, inviting the reader to a personal, prayerful reflection on each theme.

The reader will also note that I begin each chapter with a "vignette" that includes a personal approach to "living the gospel" about a variety of people from different vocations and lifestyles. Each of these individuals has integrated his or her spiritual journey with some concrete action or activity that promotes Christ's mission to the world. I found many common features in their daily routine, no matter their profession or vocation. Although they were all very active, involved and engaged in a variety of pursuits, each spent significant time each day in prayer, usually reflecting on the Scriptures, especially the prophets of the Hebrew Scriptures and Jesus, the supreme teacher and prophet of "contemplation and action."

I am most grateful to Dr. Patricia Schoelles, S.S.J., Rev. William Graf, Dr. Marvin Mich, Mark Hare and Rev. William Spilly, who all reviewed the manuscript and provided helpful corrections and suggestions. Their enthusiastic encouragement to complete the book was also most helpful and appreciated. I am also indebted to Frank Cunningham, publisher of Ave Maria Press, who provided many helpful suggestions for the manuscript and likewise gave much encouragement for this project.

We face a paradox as regards to our Christian faith today. As one writer says: "[A]lthough the culture is nominally Christian, the values of our society are appearing as more and more antithetical to those of the gospel. Reading the signs of the time can jar us into seeing the striking oppositions between cultural wisdom and Christian wisdom."[9] The reflections provided are obviously not exhaustive in their presentation of the themes, nor do they claim to be the only way that the gospel can be preached and lived in the world today. They are one way, based on the social teachings of the church, which draw on the life and message of Jesus Christ.

Abbreviations

C.C.C.	*Catechism of the Catholic Church*
G.S.	*Gaudium et Spes (The Church in the Modern World)*
L.G.	*Lumen Gentium (Dogmatic Constitution on the Church)*
N.C.C.B.	National Conference of Catholic Bishops
U.S.C.C.	United States Catholic Conference
U.S.C.C.B.	United States Conference of Catholic Bishops

Chapter One:
Care for God's Creation

"In our day, there is a growing awareness
that world peace is threatened not only by
the arms race, regional conflicts and continued injustices among peoples and
nations, but also by a lack of due respect
for nature, by the plundering of natural
resources and by a progressive decline in
the quality of life."

—*John Paul II*

*Earl C. is a crusty eighty-three-year-old father of two grown
children who speaks bluntly and to the point. He was born in
Rochester, New York, where he grew up in a typical middle
class family. After attending a Catholic grammar school and
Benjamin Franklin High School, he went to the University of
Rochester where he obtained a B.S. in chemical engineering in
1942. He worked for all his adult life at Mixing Equipment
Company in a variety of capacities including sales and the*

production of technical reference books in metallurgy. He has been married for fifty-seven years to his wife, Leda (Lee).

He admits that he was not active in church beyond weekly attendance at Mass for most of his life. Then in the 1960s, with the liturgical changes implemented by the Second Vatican Council, he became a eucharistic minister, lector and usher, the later until "it began to cut into my golf game."

A breakthrough came when he was invited and accepted working on a social ministry committee for his parish. The committee was at first charged with fund raising and disbursement of funds for worthy local charities. Then after a few years, at the request of the pastor, the committee members were asked to get out to the sites where the charities were located and connect projects and organizations with people's faces and their needs. This launched him into a long-standing association with Dimitri House, a men's homeless shelter in the inner city, where Earl for several years has helped serve two meals and provide hospitality for overnight accommodations at the shelter once a month. He has also become active at St. Martin's Soup Kitchen, a facility operated by an inner-city parish, serving a hot meal daily. The first day he arrived to volunteer, Earl asked "what is the hardest job here?" and has been slicing onions one day a week for several years.

Perhaps the greatest blessing to Earl has been serving as a eucharistic minister at a local hospital each Sunday where he especially enjoys visits to the cardiac unit. "Being there a couple of times myself for heart surgery, I know what they're worried about and I can talk to them and give them the Lord and some encouragement." Often the nurses in the ward ask Earl to speak to patients, Catholics and others, whom they believe need a boost and Earl's "shoot from the hip" clear advice and wisdom. He likes to pray with the patients when asked.

Earl prays every night before he goes to bed, using some devotional books that have sustained him through the years. He often reflects on the gospel imperative, "Do unto others what you would have them do unto you." A priest once reminded him that "to whom much has been given, much will be required" and he firmly believes that God has greatly blessed him and he must now "give return on the investment."

Recently an international team on the environment issued a sobering report: "Human demand may well have exceeded the biosphere's regenerative capacity since the 1980s."[1] In 1961, the public demand amounted to 70 percent of the planet's regenerative capacity, the study had determined. By 1999, the number had grown to 120 percent. Today humanity's demands are about 25 percent over budget. The researchers pointed out the need for human demand to stay within the amount that nature can supply. The report, published in the *Proceedings of the National Academy of Science*, identified the resources as coming from croplands, mines, forests, seas, rivers, and air. Some resources, indicated the report, are replenished naturally. Others, like oil, gas, and coal—are nonrenewable, at least in a human timeframe. A few natural systems such as agricultural soils, are being damaged beyond recovery. The leader of the think tank on sustainability, an organization called "Redefining Progress in Oakland, California," said, "We may have to prepare for ecological bankruptcy." Three years ago when the study ended it was estimated that there was a "20 percent overshoot" in demand, meaning that 1.2 earths would be needed to regenerate what humanity used. Today, the leader of the study stated, it would take 1.25.

It is clear that there are many ethical considerations that are inextricably linked to today's ecological crisis. In order for a concentrated and concerted effort to resolve the issues, it will be helpful to be grounded in a common moral perspective. Christians begin with a view of the world order based on revelation. It is in the book of Genesis that one finds a recurring theme and refrain that shows God's response to all that he had created: "God looked at everything he had made, and found it very good" (Gn 1:31a). The biblical writer shows how the first human creatures created by God, called to exercise dominion over the rest of creation, destroyed its harmony by sin. "All of creation became subject to futility, waiting in a mysterious way to be set free and to obtain a glorious liberty together with all the children of God (cf. Rom 8:20–21)."[2]

> God created man in his image;
>   in the image he created him;
>   male and female he created them.
>   God blessed them, saying: "Be fertile and
> multiply; fill the earth and subdue it. Have
> dominion over the fish of the sea, the birds
> of the air, and all the living things that
> move on the earth." God also said: "See, I
> give you every seed-bearing plant all over
> the earth and every tree that has seed-
> bearing fruit on it to be your food; and to
> all the animals of the land, all the birds of
> the air, and all the living creatures that
> crawl on the ground, I give all the green
> plants for food." And so it happened. God
> looked at everything he had made, and he
> found it very good (Gn 1:27–31a).

The biblical story of creation demonstrates some fundamental understandings of God's creation and humanity's response. "When man turns his back on the Creator's plan, he provokes a disorder which has inevitable repercussions on the rest of the created order. If man is not at peace with God, then earth itself cannot be at peace."[3]

Reflection: Our efforts to serve the poor and vulnerable must be accompanied by concrete efforts to address the causes of human suffering and injustice.

Saint Francis of Assisi had great respect for God's beauty as revealed in creation. The general outline of his life is quite well known. He was born in 1182, son of a cloth merchant, Pietro Bernardone, and his wife Pica, in a small town in the Umbrian Valley. He grew up relatively wealthy with ambition to be a knight similar to the legendary knight-errants of the court of King Arthur. While engaged in battle with Assisi's neighboring city, Perugia, he was taken prisoner. When finally released and back in Assisi, he spent a year recovering from an illness. Both experiences—the captivity and sickness—caused him to reflect on the direction of his life. While contemplating another foray into battle as a knight while encamped in the city of Spoleto, he heard a voice inviting him to service. "Francis, is it better to serve the Lord or the servant?" "Oh, sir, the Lord, of course."[4] He is told to return to Assisi where he will be told what to do. He spends a year in prayer, attempting to discern God's will. As he reflects on his life, and the values of the world around him, God's plan for him becomes clear. One day he hears the voice of God speaking to him as he prays before a crucifix in a dilapidated church, San Damiano. "Francis, go and repair my house which, as you see, is falling into ruins." Although initially interpreted by Francis to mean the repair of the ruined church before him, it becomes clearer that it is God's whole household that must be restored. Leaving home after stripping himself publicly of his clothes (and old self) he lives his dream as a knight, but now for God's kingdom. "Francis immediately begins in earnest to live the Gospel literally and without compromise, and the authenticity of his life begins to attract others."[5] Gathering a community of like-minded followers, drawn to his charisma and simplicity, Francis roams the countryside, preaching and healing, working in the fields and begging.

Many people today feel attracted to Francis. Besides those who have assumed a vowed life as Franciscan religious, many Christians admire Francis's ideals and seek to incorporate them into their own life. Two esteemed features of Francis's spirituality were his love for poverty and for his respect for creation ("Lady Poverty" and "Mother Earth"). Poverty for Francis was to live in total dependence upon God. "For Saint Francis, living in the radical insecurity of poverty was the ultimate act of living faith in the providence of God and the promises of Christ."[6] Creation was providential guidance, a "sign of the presence of God, and more specifically, of the presence of Christ in the created world."[7] In 1979, Pope John Paul II proclaimed Saint Francis of Assisi, quite appropriately, as the patron for those who promote ecology. "As a friend of the poor who was loved by God's creatures, Saint Francis invited all of creation—animals, plants, natural forces, even Brother Sun and Sister Moon—to give honor and praise to the Lord."[8] The saint saw the world as a gift from the Creator to the creature.

"Francis was incapable of seeing the world of creation as a mere thing for the use of humanity. He insisted on the integrity of all creatures in the scheme of things."[9] Flowing from Francis's appreciation of nature was a profound sense of gratitude for what God has given to us:

> For Saint Francis, God is the perfect giver because He is the gift. God gives us the world, life and, for Francis the Christian, "His only begotten Son." The beauty of the world and the intrinsic dignity of every individual is guaranteed by its rootedness in God. To understand that fact prevents one from ever calling Francis a pantheist; Francis did not mistake the gift for the giver.[10]

Francis's love for God's creation was intimately linked to his appreciation for his poverty—the poverty that helps us see all we have and are as God's gift. "A sense of this kind of poverty makes us grateful for the gift of creation, helps us to be sensitive to the needs of others, and allows us a closer identification with that Christ who became 'poor for our sake.'"[11]

In 1224, Francis composed a hymn to God that praises creation, that teaches how one can find God when "He finds you loving the world He has created and redeemed."[12]

> Most high, all-powerful, all good, Lord!
> All praise is yours, all glory, all [honor]
> And all blessing.
> To you alone, Most High, do they belong
>   No mortal lips are worthy
>   To pronounce your name.

All praise be yours, my Lord, through all
that you have made,
And first, my lord Brother Sun,
Who brings the day; and light you give
us through him.
How beautiful is he, how radiant in all his
splendor!
Of you, Most High he bears the likeness.
All praise be yours, my Lord, through
Sister Moon and Stars;
In the heavens you have made them,
bright
And precious and fair.
All praise be yours, My Lord through
Brothers Wind and Air,
And fair and stormy, all the weather's
moods,
By which you cherish all that you have
made.
All praise be yours, my Lord, through
Sister Water,
So useful, lowly, precious and pure.
All praise be yours, my Lord, through
Brother Fire,
Through whom you brighten up the
night.
How beautiful he is, how gay! Full of
power and strength
All praise be yours, my Lord, through
Sister Earth, our mother,
Who feeds us in her sovereignty and
produces
Various fruits and colored flowers
and herbs. . . .[13]

"The poor man of Assisi" says John Paul II, "gives us striking witness that when we are at peace with God we are better able to devote ourselves to building up that peace with all creation which is inseparable from peace among all peoples."[14]

Francis built on an image of creation and prayerful respect for God's gifts as seen in the Hebrew and Christian Scriptures. In the book of Genesis, God looked at all that he had created and saw that it was very good. The psalmist was deeply aware of the power and wonder of God as revealed in his handiwork:

> You have spread out the heavens like a
>   tent-cloth;
> You have constructed your palace upon
>   the waters.
> You make the clouds your chariot;
> You travel on the wings of the wind.
> You make the winds your messengers,
>   and flaming fire your ministers.
>   (Ps 104:2–4)

God has established a beautiful order and rhythm to the universe. In rich imagery the same psalm goes on to show the Creator's design and handiwork:

> You made the moon to mark the seasons;
>   the sun knows the hour of its
>   setting.
> You bring darkness, and it is night;
>   then all the beasts of the forest roam
>   about;
> Young lions roar for the prey
>   and seek their food from God.
> When the sun rises, they withdraw

and couch in their dens,
Man goes forth to his work
    and to his tillage till the evening.
How manifold are your works, O LORD!
    In wisdom you have wrought them
        all (Ps 104:19–24a).

Some psalms, explains Walter Brueggemann, can be classified as "descriptive hymns." ". . . [T]hey are statements that describe a happy, blessed state in which the speakers are grateful for, and confident in the abiding, reliable gifts of life that are long standing from time past and will endure for time to come."[15] He would further describe the psalms as expressions of *creation faith.* "They affirm that the world is a well-ordered, reliable, and life-giving system because God has ordained it that way and continues to preside effectively over the process." Or as C. S. Lewis describes it: ". . . [B]elieving in Creation, is to see Nature not as a mere datum but an achievement. Some of the Psalmists are delighted with its mere solidity and permanence."[16] Such an affirmation of God, recognizing His creative powers and his watchful protection over what He had created, gave the people of Israel peace of mind. "[The psalms of creation] articulate and maintain a 'sacred canopy' under which the community of faith can live out its life with freedom from anxiety."[17] For example, in Psalm 148 we hear Israel's joyous praise, in gratitude to God for the gift of his creation.

Praise the LORD from the heavens,
    praise him in the heights;
Praise him, all you his angels,
    praise him, all you his hosts.
Praise him, sun and moon;
    praise him, all you shining stars.

> Praise him, you highest heavens,
>   and you waters above the heavens.
> Let them praise the name of the LORD,
>   for he commanded and they were
> created;
> He established them forever and ever;
>   he gave them a duty which shall not pass
>   away (vv.1–6).

All of creation should return thanks and praise to God, since creation demonstrates God's continued giving. Israel could see each day, in the mountains and plains surrounding them, the rain and the sun, and the stars and the moon, that God was faithful and provident. God's faithfulness is a judgment made not by profound theological reflection, but rather by experience: "experience of daily reliability, evidence from the simple facts of being nourished and having the necessities of life provided."[18]

Psalm 104 speaks forcefully of the splendor of creation—its order, symmetry and majesty:

> Bless the LORD, O my soul!
>   O LORD, my God, you are great indeed!
> You are clothed with majesty and glory,
>   robed in light as with a cloak.
> You have spread out the heavens like a
>   tent-cloth;
>   you have constructed your palace upon
>   the waters.
> You make the clouds your chariot;
>   you travel on the wings of the wind.
> You make the winds your messengers,
>   and flaming fire your ministers (vv. 1–4).

The whole world, prays the psalm, is dependent upon God's care.

> They all look to you
> to give them food in due time.
> When you give it to them, they gather it;
> when you open your hand, they are
> filled with good things (vv. 27–28).

The created world is indeed impressive. But it still must depend on God. "The world is well-ordered and reliable. But on its own, it has no possibility of survival or well-being. All of that is a daily gift."[19] The speaker then goes on to spontaneous wonder, gratitude and praise, delighting in God's goodness:

> May the glory of the LORD endure forever;
> may the LORD be glad in his works!
> He who looks upon the earth, and it
> trembles;
> who touches the mountains and they
> smoke!
> I will sing to the LORD all my life;
> I will sing praise to my God while I live.
> Pleasing to him be my theme;
> I will be glad in the LORD (vv. 31–34).

The world is a gift from God. But God has not surrendered his sovereignty. The conclusion of this psalm ("may sinners cease from the earth and may the wicked be no more") reminds the people that they are responsible for the good use of the gift of creation.

Psalm 33 speaks of the new world of creation, ordered by God, and how Israel is instructed to praise the Creator.

Exult, you just, in the LORD;
   praise from the upright is fitting
Give thanks to the LORD on the harp;
   with the ten-stringed lyre chant his
      praises.
Sing to him a new song;
   pluck the strings skillfully, with shouts of
      gladness.
For upright is the word of the LORD,
   and all his works are trustworthy.
He loves justice and right;
   of the kindness of the LORD the earth is
      full (vv. 1–5).

The next verses describe the power of God's word
(mentioned in v. 4) to bring creation into being.
"Creation by God's word is only one mode of creation,
but it is the most awesome and majestic."[20]

By the word of the LORD the heavens were
      made;
   by the breath of the mouth all their host.
He gathers the waters of the sea as a flask:
   in cellars he confines the deep (vv. 6–7).

God utterly and totally controls the world. The fact that
he can contain the waters of the earth in a flask shows
the immensity of his strength. The natural response
from God's creatures must be awe and respect, "fear
and trembling" at his unquestionable power:

Let all the earth fear the LORD;
   let all who dwell in the world revere
      him.
For he spoke and it was made;
   he commanded, and it stood forth.

> The LORD brings to nought the plans of
> nations;
> he foils the designs of peoples.
> But the plan of the LORD stands forever;
> the design of his heart, through all gener-
> ations.
> Happy the nation whose God is the LORD,
> the people he has chosen for his own
> inheritance (vv. 8–12).

God watches over his people, and in fact all creation.
"Israel need not be anxious, because God's rule is not in
doubt and will not be challenged."[21]

> From heaven the Lord looks down;
> he sees all mankind.
> From his fixed throne he beholds
> all who dwell on the earth,
> He who fashioned the heart of each,
> he who knows all their works (vv. 3–15).

By observing God's care for his creation, Israel can
rejoice in hope. Israel will not be abandoned. God is
steadfast. It is in him, and not wealth or power that
Israel must place its hope:

> A king is not saved by a mighty army,
> nor is a warrior delivered by great
> strength.
> Useless is the horse for safety;
> great though its strength, it cannot pro-
> vide escape.
> But see, the eyes of the LORD are upon
> those who fear him,
> upon those who hope for his kindness,
> To deliver them from death

and preserve them in spite of famine (vv. 16–19).

In Psalm 8, we hear praise to the Creator God. The human person is described as having a special role in the governance of creation.

> O LORD, our Lord,
>   how glorious is your name over all the
>   earth!
>   You have exalted your majesty above the
>   heavens.
> Out of the mouths of babes and sucklings
>   you have fashioned praise because of
>   your foes,
>   to silence the hostile and the vengeful.
> When I behold your heavens, the work of
>   your fingers.
>   the moon and the stars which you set in
>   place—
> What is man that you should be mindful
>   of him;
>   or the son of man that you should care
>   for him (vv. 1–5)?

Humankind is mentioned in terms of glory and honor. "When one looks up at the sky, and all the stars which are His work, it seems strange that He should be concerned at all with such things as man. Yet, in fact, though He has made us inferior to the celestial beings, He has, down here on earth, given us extraordinary honor—made us lords of all the other creatures."[22] Humankind has dominion over the other creatures not unlike God.

Pope John Paul II has expressed concern about the emerging crisis caused by humanity's lack of appreciation of the created world: "In our day, there is a growing awareness that world peace is threatened not only by the arms race, regional conflicts and continued injustices among peoples and nations, but also by a lack of *due respect for nature*, by the plundering of natural resources and by a progressive decline in the quality of life."[23] The possible devastating effects of a lack of concern becomes quickly obvious: "The sense of precariousness and insecurity that such a situation engenders is a seedbed for collective selfishness, disregard for others and dishonesty."[24]

On November 14, 1991, the U.S. bishops issued *Renewing the Earth: An Invitation to Reflection and Action on the Environment in Light of Catholic Social Teaching*, which discusses the connection between Catholic social teaching and care for the environment. Highlighted are the proper use and sharing of the goods of the earth; what will be passed on to future generations and the need to live in harmony with all God's creation. "If the world of today would return to the spirit of praise found in the Bible and in all true disciples of Christ, it would not be too difficult to resolve the ecological crisis. . . ."[25]

One does not have to look far to see the effects of the crisis: smog in cities, chemicals in water and on food, eroded topsoil, loss of valuable wetlands, radioactive and toxic waste lacking adequate disposal sites and threats to the health of industrial and farm workers, just to name a few. The problems are extensive: acid rain, greenhouse gases and chlorofluorocarbons. But environmental damage is done not only by large corporations, insensitive to the environment. Citizens with patterns of over-consumption and wastefulness also contribute to the problem.

---

*Reflection: We are called to
transform our hearts and our
social structures, to renew the
face of the earth.*

It is not the scientific, but rather the moral analysis that will be most beneficial as the church's contribution to the issues. "The Church has as one of its primary functions the educative role of helping believers and other people of good will form their consciences so that they can see environmental issues as having moral content."[26] The bishops address this issue of ecology not as scientists or experts. "There will be legitimate differences and debate over how these challenging moral principles are applied to concrete situations."[27] They come to these complex environmental problems as pastors who see a moral and religious crisis. They come with a prophetic witness with ethical considerations, e.g., our responsibility to make sure that succeeding generations have the necessary goods of the earth. "Care for the earth is not just an Earth Day slogan, it is a requirement of our faith. We are called to protect people and the planet, living our faith in relationship with all of God's creation."[28]

The bishops see a social justice connection with ecology. For example, they link together issues of ecology and poverty. It is often the poor, the bishops would claim, whose lands and environment suffer due to ecological blight. Barbara Kohnen develops this theme:

> While important, personal lifestyle
> changes in the richer nations and commu-
> nity development projects in developing

nations cannot by themselves create long-term sustainable economic development. The global economy and poverty operate at many levels, from the international marketplace to the village. International economic forces often can benefit the rich while undermining the livelihoods of the poor through low commodity prices, crushing external debt burdens, volatile capital markets, and misallocated aid. At the local level, unequal rights to land and productive resources, inadequate provision of health care and education, and the inability of the poorest people to influence decisions affecting their lives contribute to poverty. Corrupt or unaccountable governments can misuse public funds or marginalize the poor in the name of economic progress.[29]

All that has been created by God is a gift that is given by the Creator for the benefit of all people. "When man turns his back on the Creator's plan, he provokes a disorder which has inevitable repercussions on the rest of the created order."[30] It was not one nation, culture or society that received the gifts of God's creation. Rather, God's gifts are intended for all. The goodness of creation belongs not to just a select few, but to the whole human family. "This environmental challenge has fundamental moral and ethical dimensions that cannot be ignored."[31]

*Reflection: We cannot celebrate
a faith we do not practice.*

The whole earth is God's dwelling. Many come to faith as they marvel at the wonderful designs of God's handiwork. "God speaks to man through the visible creation. The material cosmos is so presented to man's intelligence that he can read the traces of its Creator. Light and darkness, wind and fire, water and earth, the tree and its fruit speak of God and symbolize both his greatness and his nearness. "[32] The psalmist expresses constant amazement and delight at what the Creator has fashioned.

Jesus himself often used the imagery of created nature in his parables to teach the truth of the kingdom, in his parables and in his examples. "The sower went out to sow his seeds"; "the kingdom of heaven is like a tiny mustard seed." Paul's letters teach that creation manifests God power.[33] It is God from whom and through whom all things come into being (Rom 11:36). Christ is the principle of all creation, the first—born in whom everything in heaven and earth is created, both visible and invisible (Col 1:15 ff.). God has created the world through his Son, bearing all things through his powerful Word (Heb 1:2, ff.).

The Gospel itself according to John Paul II, is the *celebration of the joy of creation.* "God who in creating saw that His creation was good (cf. Gn 1:1–25), is the source of joy for all creatures, and above all humankind. God the Creator seems to say to all creation: 'It is good that you exist.' And His joy spreads especially through the 'good news' according to which *good is greater than all that is evil in the world.*"[34] Creation is entrusted to humankind as a duty, representing "not a source of suffering but *the foundation of a creative existence in the world.* A person who believes in the essential goodness of all creation is capable of discovering all the secrets of creation. . . ."[35] One who has come to recognize the goodness of creation and befriended it, can help to develop creation in a positive way.

At the heart of the Christian faith is love of neighbor. The ecological crisis can be addressed as our call to love our neighbor, extended beyond this world. Our careful tending to the natural resources at our disposal is a bequest to those who will come after us. "Man's dominion over inanimate and other living beings is not absolute; it is limited by concern for the quality of life of his neighbor, including generations to come; it requires a religious respect for the integrity of creation."[36]

---

*Reflection: We cannot proclaim
a gospel we do not live.*

People are called to make choices for an equitable and sustainable future in which all peoples can share in the bounty of the earth. "We must be adorers in spirit and truth, gifted with wisdom and discernment and creative in an affirmative sense."[37] We are invited to look carefully at our lifestyles to see how we may be contributing to the destruction or neglect of our environment. "Those responsible for business enterprises are responsible to society for the economic and ecological effects of their operations."[38]

Many prophets within our midst are inviting us to a simpler lifestyle. In some ways, the environmental crisis is an invitation to an extended examination of conscience, a call to renewal and a change of heart. First, as a nation, we are called to consider the impact of our choices on nature, and subsequently on ourselves. "Respect for life, and above all for the dignity of the human person, is the ultimate guiding norm for any sound economic, industrial or scientific progress."[39] For each Christian, such a self-examination in this area can be fruitful. "A new asceticism beckons us to a new kind of fasting, renunciation, and temperance as part of a lifestyle marked by simplicity and the joys inherent in it."[40] The fact that we own property does not diminish our need to see it as gift and to exercise stewardship. "The right to private property, acquired by work or received from others by inheritance or gift, does not do away with the original gift of the earth to the whole of mankind. The universal destination of goods remains primordial, even if the promotion of the common good requires respect for the right to private property and its exercise."[41] Hopefully, the state can provide its citizens freedom from dangerous pollutants and toxic wastes. "The right to a safe environment is ever more insistently presented today as a right that must be included in an updated Charter of Human Rights."[42]

> You, O God, Majestic Creator, are the origin of all life.
> Nothing can exclude itself from your creative influence.
> You are wonderful in your words, and in your sovereignty.
> Amazed, I contemplate the perfection of the world you created for human beings.
> You are unmatched in your power and in your goodness.
> O Lord, you direct like a conductor the orchestration of a storm, and you shape like a sculptor the petals of a flower.
> You are prodigious in your majesty and in your wisdom.
> Lord, you have fashioned human beings to accept the challenge of nature and to be your voice in creation.

O Lord and King, Majestic Creator, you
have made your mystery transparent in
the world you have created.
I worship you in your creation and in your
providence.
Amen.[43]

Reflection Questions:

1. What are our moral obligations to succeeding generations from an ecological perspective?

2. How can parents best teach their children about ecological aspects of their Christian faith?

3. How best may business and community leaders
address the issue of ecology in their sphere of influence?

4. Are there aspects of my lifestyle that need to be exam-
ined and changed as I reflect on the ecological problems
that face us at the present time?

5. How can I best impact those involved in various levels of government with concerns about environmental
issues? How can I best be kept informed about important developments in this area?

6. What is the relationship between our liturgical cele-
brations and care for God's creation?

Chapter Two:
Life and the Dignity of the Human Person

"The right to life means the right to be
born and then continue to live until one's
natural end: 'As long as I live, I have the
right to live.'"

— *John Paul II*

*Fr. Jim H. has been a priest of the Diocese of Rochester for
thirty years. He was born in East Rochester, New York, on
March 20, 1947, and after attending McQuaid Jesuit High
School, decided to undertake studies for the priesthood. The
movement towards his vocation he believes began as early as
grammar school, when a religious sister took her students to
church during Lent and prayed with them the Stations of the
Cross. He says that he was so moved by the depth of Christ's
sacrifice that he began to consider a return in kind. Eventually,
the sacrifice became a vocation as a priest.*

He has had assignments in a variety of parishes as both an associate pastor and pastor in the Diocese of Rochester. Although his assignments have included rural areas, suburban, and city, he now serves as pastor to two parishes in Clyde, and Savannah, New York, approximately fifty miles from Rochester. In addition to the typical parish duties, he has devoted much of his ministry to the protection of life issues. In 1968, while in college, he attended a lecture by a medical doctor working against abortions. So struck was he by the slides of unborn children included in the presentation, that he began to orient his priorities to the protection of life in the womb. In 1969 he joined one of the first right-to-life organizations in New York State and soon became a member of the board. In 1976 he was asked by his bishop to help create the first diocesan medico-moral committee. A struggle that he recounts during these years is his efforts to expand the vision of those who worked in anti-abortion ministry to see how the same basic principles should be applied to the death penalty and war issues. Cardinal Joseph Bernardin of Chicago would become a national spokesperson for this "seamless garment, consistent life ethic."

One of Jim's special interests has been Project Rachel, a network of professional counselors and priests trained to provide one-on-one psychological and spiritual care for those suffering because of an abortion. Founded in 1984 by Victoria Thorn in Milwaukee, Project Rachel today has over 140 programs in various Catholic dioceses in the United States as well as other countries. Jim believes that one of the surest proofs of the dignity of the unborn child is a grieving mother after an abortion.

Jim traces at least part of his desire to minister in pro-life issues to a sensitivity and compassion he has always had for the marginalized. He has interiorized this sensitivity by integrating his spiritual life with a vision of the compassionate

God. The Word made flesh affirms the dignity of the individual.

Jim spends one hour a day in prayer, as a required priority, which he believes keeps his work in life issues from becoming just an "ideology." This quiet time includes centering prayer, the liturgy of the hours (breviary) and meditation on Scripture. It is while praying that he senses that even in his sinfulness, he is loved by God, as an individual and unique creation of God. Such a perception, he believes, lays the groundwork for any work in social justice—affirming each individual as a unique gift from a loving God.

In Matthew's gospel, Jesus is portrayed as a sage surrounded by followers who come to the Master with great anticipation, eagerly listening to him preaching the kingdom, "God's future display of power and judgment and eventual establishment of his rule over all creation."[1] Some come to him with dashed hopes as they observe the cruelty of Roman conquest, their dreams for autonomy and freedom crushed. Some come with a questioning heart, wondering what has become of the vision of their ancestors and the arrival of a messiah who would fulfill the longing of restless hearts. Some have basic needs: they come to the wandering carpenter with a variety of afflictions and various ailments asking for miraculous cures, signs of God's benevolence. Some simply ask for food as they have followed him for many days hungry and weary from the Palestinian heat. "Jesus spoke to [people] who were desperately trying to find God, and who were desperately trying to be good and who finding the tasks impossible, and who were driven to weariness and to despair."[2]

Jesus issues an invitation that has provided encouragement for centuries since: "Come to me all you who are weary and find life burdensome, and I will refresh you. Take my yoke upon your shoulders and learn from me, for I am gentle and humble of heart. Your souls will find rest, for my yoke is easy and my burden light" (Mt 11:28-30).

Much of Jesus' ministry consisted of affirmation and encouragement. He extended an invitation to those who are exhausted from their search for the truth. "It is Jesus' claim that the weary search for God ends in himself."[3] Contrary to the Scribes and Pharisees, who bound heavy burdens too hard to carry on others' shoulders (Mt 23:4), Jesus alleviated burdens and gave needed rest. His power to heal many times included simply helping people appreciate their own dignity as children of God. He realized that such an awareness in the hearts of his disciples could also bring forth miracles.

An affirmation of another's inherent dignity cannot help but flow into actions of love towards others. Parables such as the story of the Good Samaritan (Lk 10:25–37) teach us that love of neighbor must have an expansive quality, directed not only to kinspeople. The parable was told in answer to the question by an expert in the law, "who is my neighbor?" responding to Jesus' question about the law and requirements for gaining everlasting life. The lawyer had correctly identified the key elements: love of God and love of neighbor. But, needing to justify himself, he wanted a specific, legal rendering of "neighbor." The answer, provided by Jesus, is in the form of a parable that involves a despised Samaritan who comes to the Jewish victim's rescue. The unexpected twist dramatically expands the definition of neighbor beyond the commonly understood one of that time: one's fellow countrymen. Unlike the priest and the

Levite who simply passed by the wounded traveler, the Samaritan is a true neighbor to the man in need. The only criterion needed for the Samaritan to give aid was that he had encountered someone in desperate need. "Who was the true neighbor?" "The one who showed mercy." "Neighbor is not just your like-minded in-group."[4] Those who show compassion with a generous heart—theirs is the Kingdom of God.

Reflection: In the Catholic social vision, the human person is central.

A Christian anthropology understands each human person as being made in the image and likeness of God. As recorded in Genesis 1:27: "God created man in his own image; in the divine image he created him; male and female he created them." The manner whereby the human being is created differs in style and substance from the rest of God's creation. This is seen clearly by the way "God involves himself directly in what is done. Where formerly there had been an impersonal 'Let there be . . .' for the creation of the heavens, earth and the animals, there is now an intensely personal 'Let us make . . .'[5] for the creation of the person. The human being will have a role that no other creature can fulfill. ". . . [I]t must follow . . . that God had established with this creature alone [the human being] the kind of 'personal' relationship that would enable him to get through to him and communicate his will to him."[6]

The mystery of the Christian faith known as the "Incarnation," God made human in Jesus Christ, reveals the sacrality of the human person. "The Word became flesh" (Jn 1:14) is a distinctive belief of Christianity. "The unique and altogether singular event of the Incarnation of the Son of God does not mean that Jesus Christ is part God and part man, nor does it imply that he is the result of a confused mixture of the divine and human. He became truly man while remaining truly God. Jesus Christ is truly God and truly man."[7] The Word becomes flesh to make us partakers in the divine life. "Our human dignity is fully revealed in Christ, whose sacrifice eloquently expresses *how precious we are* in the eyes of the Creator. Tarnished by sin, our dignity is definitively restored through the cross and shown forth in the resurrection."[8] When a sense of a transcendent yet imminent God is lost in a society, it frequently results in a devalued sense of the human person as well.

> *Reflection: All people are a reflection of the image of God and thus all human life, at all its stages from conception through death, is sacred.*

Racism is an evil that continues in society today. It is not uncommon to hear complaints or the sentiment that too much is being given to racial minorities by way of affirmative action programs or other initiatives that seek to address long standing imbalances in minority representation and government-funded programs. Christians are called upon to influence the attitudes of others by expressly rejecting racial stereotypes and by becoming more sensitive as to how social structures can sometimes inhibit the economic, educational, and social advancement of people, especially minorities.

Many Christians who have reflected on the criminal justice system have called on their fellow citizens to reflect on capital punishment. Pope John Paul II in his encyclical *Evangelium Vitae, The Gospel of Life,* invites all people of good will to ponder on the most basic affirmation of life: "Thou shall not kill." Facing the myriad moral questions that flow from this issue, the Christian must consider the plan of God for each individual and for society as a whole, as taught by the scriptures and tradition. Does the need for society to address a serious wrong that has been committed, such as the taking of an innocent life by deliberate intention, require the taking of another life—that of the perpetrator of the crime? Granted the need for society to defend its citizens and values by an adequate punishment that prevents future crimes, John Paul stresses an additional requirement: that an opportunity for conversion of heart be offered. Only in cases of absolute necessity must life be taken and capital punishment utilized. Such cases, the pope insists, are rare enough to be considered practically "non-existent." "A sign of hope is the increasing recognition that the dignity of human life must never be taken away, even in the case of someone who has done great evil. Modern society has the means of protecting itself, without definitely denying criminals the chance to reform. I renew the appeal I made most recently . . . for a consensus to end the death penalty, which is both cruel and unnecessary."[9]

Several factors should be considered as the issue of capital punishment is discussed:

- The death penalty is racially biased; nearly 90 percent of persons executed were convicted of killing whites, although people of color make up over half of all homicide victims in the United States;

- Capital punishment does not deter crime: states that have the death penalty have higher civilian murder rates than those that do not;

- Capital punishment kills innocent people; in
  the last twenty years, in 350 capital convictions, it was later revealed that the convicted
  person did not commit the crime. Of these,
  twenty people were executed.[10]

The bishops of the United States have called for a careful and prayerful reflection on capital punishment. They
identify areas of concern when capital punishment is the
decision of the state: is this decision the best way society
may defend itself from those who have taken a human
life? Will the execution of violators of those who have
taken a life protect the lives of those who must defend
society as law enforcement officers? What is owed to the
families of those who have lost a loved one at the hands
of a murderer? In his statement on the occasion of the
execution of Timothy McVeigh, convicted in the bomb-
ing of the Alfred P. Murrah Federal Building in
Oklahoma City on April 19, 1995, the then President of
the United States Conference of Catholic Bishops,
Bishop Joseph Fiorenza, stated: "In an age where respect
for life is threatened in so many ways, we believe it is
important to emphasize that human life is a gift from
God, and no one or any government should presume to
kill God's gift. Rather all of us have the responsibility to
protect human life from conception to natural death."[11]

Although Catholic teaching has accepted the principle
that the state has the right to defend its citizenry against
the criminal who would take a life and inflict harm
against the innocent, the bishops continue to ask, as
does Pope John Paul, whether capital punishment is jus-
tifiable under present circumstances. On Good Friday,
April 2, 1999, the Administrative Board of the United
States Conference of Catholic Bishops issued an urgent
appeal for the end of the death penalty. As they noted in
their statement: "Sadly, many Americans—including

many Catholics—still support the death penalty out of understandable fear of crime and horror at so many lives lost through criminal violence. We hope that they will come to see, as we have, that more violence is not the answer."[12]

The bishops call Catholics and all people of good will to join with them in working to end the death penalty. "Through education, through advocacy, and through prayer and contemplation on the life of Jesus, we must commit ourselves to a persistent and principled witness against the death penalty, against a culture of death, and for the Gospel of Life."[13] As Cardinal Theodore McCarrick stated bluntly on April 18, 2002, as chair of the U.S.C.C.B. Domestic Policy Committee: "The report that at least 100 people have now been found to be innocent of the crimes that put them on death row are 100 reasons to turn away from capital punishment. The 101st reason is not what was done to them, but what is being done to us."[14]

Reflection: The human person is the clearest reflection of God among us.

The starting point for Pope John Paul's approach to issues concerning life is the sacredness of the individual's human dignity which he teaches must be the foundation for a moral vision for society. We live in an age of surprising contradiction, where the inviolable rights of the person are proclaimed yet the basic right to life is being trampled or even denied.

Sometimes it appears today that life is valued only to the extent that it brings pleasure. When a life is no longer capable of youthful vigor and begins to undergo the natural developments of the aging process, sometimes questions are raised relative to its efficacy and value. Pope John Paul II, in a "Letter to the Elderly," speaks of the natural aging process: ". . . [S]cripture maintains a very positive vision of the value of life. Man remains for ever made 'in the image of God' (cf. Gn 1:26), and each stage of life has its own beauty and its own tasks."[15] He recounts the varied contributions of the elderly wise who contributed to God's mysterious plan as recorded in the Scriptures. He includes the journeys of Abraham, Sarah, Moses, Tobit, and Eleazor from the Hebrew Scripture; Elizabeth, Zechariah, Simeon, Anna, and Nicodemus in the Christian Scriptures. Common to these figures is "a favorable time" for bringing life to its fulfillment, the elder years, a time when "everything comes together and enables us better to grasp life's meaning and to attain 'wisdom of heart.'"[16] The people of today who likewise are in this time of life are not always respected and revered by the young, due largely to a mentality that gives priority to "usefulness" and "productivity." "Such an attitude frequently leads to contempt for the later years of life, while older people themselves are led to wonder whether their lives are still worthwhile."[17]

When a life seems destined for long-term suffering, many today question the value of prolonging suffering and wonder whether death may be the more reasonable alternative. Euthanasia can be distinguished from the decision that is sometimes made to forego an aggressive medical treatment. Sometimes when death is imminent and inevitable, it may be a proper decision made from faith to refuse forms of treatment that provide only a burdensome prolongation of life. "Discontinuing medical procedures that are burdensome, dangerous, extraordinary, or disproportionate to the expected outcome can be legitimate. Here one does not will to cause death; one's inability to impede it is merely accepted."[18] But even if death seems imminent, the ordinary care that is owed to a sick person cannot be legitimately interrupted.[19] John Paul deplores the solution that has become more and more utilized for this difficult situation: "Unfortunately, in recent years the idea of euthanasia has lost for many people the sense of horror which it naturally awakens in those who have a respect for life."[20] He would ask that certain distinctions be carefully kept in mind when the situation of lingering suffering is engaged:

> Certainly it can happen that, when grave illness involves unbearable suffering, the sick are tempted to despair and their loved ones or those responsible for their care feel compelled by a misguided compassion to consider the solution of an "easy death" as something reasonable. Here it should be kept in mind that the moral law allows the rejection of "aggressive medical treatment" and makes obligatory only those forms of treatment which fall within the normal requirements of medical care, which in the case of terminal illness seeks primarily to alleviate pain. But euthanasia, understood as directly causing the death, is another thing entirely. Regardless of intentions and circumstances, euthanasia is always an intrinsically evil act, a violation of God's law and an offense against the dignity of the human person.[21]

The antidote to the stigma of growing old and the suffering and sickness that often accompanies it is a correct perspective of eternity, for which life is a meaningful preparation in the Christian mystery. "Old age too has a proper role to play in this process of gradual maturing along the path to eternity. And this process of maturing cannot but benefit the larger society of which the elderly person is a part."[22]

To take one's own life is a rejection of God's absolute sovereignty over life and death. It is God who remains the sovereign guardian of all life. Unfortunately, and tragically, serious psychological disturbances, anguish, grave fear, and a variety of circumstances can diminish the ability of a person to act responsibly. To assist another in this process is to act unjustly. It is wrong, says John Paul II, for legislators to take upon themselves the power to decide who shall live and who shall die.

Deciding about life and death issues are very much part and parcel of living today in a democracy. It is not unusual today to see voter referenda that ask the citizens to decide by vote about issues such as euthanasia or doctor-assisted suicides. Living within a democratic society does not mean that the democratic choice, even after a vote, is a correct moral decision. The democratic state can be judged to be moral on the basis of whether or not it conforms to the moral law. Furthermore, a vote in a democracy does not guarantee that a moral vision will be implemented. It is clear, as a result of the natural law written in each person's heart, there exists an inviolable right to life for every human person. Any human law that would seek to disregard this natural law, even if approved by a majority of the citizens, does not guarantee a moral state. To the contrary, Christians are called to refuse to take part in practices that would be committing moral injustice. The Congregation for the Doctrine of the Faith, in its recent "Doctrinal Note On Some Questions Regarding the Participation of Catholics in

Political Life," reiterated the need for conformity of conscience and practice, especially for those who serve in public office: "When political activity comes up against moral principles that do not admit of exception, compromise or derogation, the Catholic commitment becomes more evident and laden with responsibility" (no. 4).

Reflection: Each person
possesses a basic human dignity
that comes from God.

Jesus came to show us our true nature as human beings. The vast crowds that came to Jesus with disease, illnesses and wants of every kind found in him someone truly concerned and empathetic. He wished to share with them the Father's love that gave their pain meaning and even value. The mission of Jesus, with the many healings that he performed showed that God was concerned for every aspect of the person's life, even physical. The constant teaching and preaching of Jesus was towards wholeness and life. Each person is called to experience this life. This gives each human a sacred dignity—that he or she is created by God in God's image and destined for everlasting life. No one is empowered to arbitrarily take life away from another. Rather, we are called as disciples to defend and promote life in all its stages.

Pope John Paul II has characterized this age as the "culture of death." He deplores the philosophy of the day that would say that a life that requires a greater acceptance, more love and care is "useless" or at least an intolerable burden that must be rejected by modern standards. He speaks, for example, of "a pro-abortion culture" which sees the life that results from a sexual encounter as an enemy to be avoided at all costs. The only solution to such a perspectives lies in a renewed appreciation of the dignity of the human person, understood to be present even in the womb.

Reflection: The test of every institution or policy is whether it enhances or threatens human life and human dignity.

John Paul has spoken eloquently and forcefully concerning the need to protect especially against the loss of innocent life. One effort is the teaching of the church that from the time that the ovum is fertilized, a life is begun that is neither that of the mother or the father, but rather the life of a new human being with its own growth. The individual must be respected and treated as a person from the moment of conception. "From the first moment of his existence, a human being must be recognized as having the rights of a person—among which is the inviolable right of every innocent being to life."[23]

It is the crime of abortion that has occupied much of the recent teaching of the church concerning issues of life. The Supreme Court of the United States, in its decision *Roe v. Wade* in 1973 decided that a woman's right to privacy included a decision to have an abortion. As a result:

- more than 1.5 million abortions are performed each year;

- more than 4,400 abortions occur daily;

- 95 percent of these abortions occur for economic or social reasons.[24]

The encyclical *Evangelium Vitae* (*The Gospel of Life*) effectively outlined a contemporary Catholic position against abortion and other offenses against the dignity of the human person. "Here the pope teaches that because human life has a sacred and inviolable character, it is always gravely immoral to destroy innocent human life."[25] John Paul is aware that the decision made by a mother for an abortion is not always made for selfish reasons, but he cannot accept that such a decision is ever morally acceptable.

Such a moral approach obviously affects the position that the church has developed towards related issues such as embryo experimentation. From a consistent perspective, the use of human embryos or fetuses can be seen as a violation of the dignity of a human person, whether such is to be used as biological material or to provide organs or tissues for transplants.

The bishops of the United States have attempted to make understandable and practicable in the United States the issues concerning life that the pope has addressed. "We believe that every person is precious, that people are more important than things, and that the measure of every institution is whether it threatens or enhances the life and dignity of the human person."[26] The bishops have noted the tragic consequences of the U.S. Supreme Court decision of 1973, *Roe v. Wade* and its companion decision *Doe v. Bolton* that effectively removed legal protection for human beings prior to birth. The bishops catalogue the unfortunate results:

- The deaths of millions whose lives were destroyed before birth and even during the very process of being born.

- Countless women traumatized so deeply by abortion that they spend years struggling to find peace, healing, and reconciliation.

- Men who grieve because they could not "choose" to protect a child they helped bring into existence.

- A society increasingly coarsened by toleration and acceptance of acts that purposely destroy human life.

The bishops also believe that a later decision of the Court, (*Planned Parenthood v. Casey*), which reaffirmed *Roe v. Wade*, was based largely on the fear that to reverse its prior decision would have undermined the court's authority. In 2000, in the court decision *Stenberg v. Carhart*, the court expanded the right to abortion to include the practice of killing during birth, "the partial birth abortion."

To live the Christian life is to commit oneself to the promotion of those values considered fundamental to the name Christian and its founder, Jesus Christ. The inalienable right to life of every innocent human individual is to be promoted and defended by civil society: "These human rights depend neither on single individuals nor on parents; nor do they represent a concession made by society and the state; they belong to human nature and are inherent in the person by virtue of the creative act from which the person took his origin."[27] The bishops have been particularly emphatic in reminding Catholics who serve in public office of their moral responsibility to defend life in all its stages. "No public official, especially one claiming to be a faithful and serious Catholic, can responsibly advocate for or actively support direct attacks on innocent life . . . no appeal to policy, procedure, majority will or pluralism ever excuses a public official from defending life to the greatest extent possible."[28] Some Catholics in the political arena may respond that the democratic state has freely elected many initiatives that support a woman's right to choose. "Those who justify their inaction on the grounds that abortion is the law of the land need to recognize that there is a higher law, the law of God. No human law can validly contradict the Commandment: 'Thou shalt not kill.'"[29] Catholic citizens, as part of the electorate in a free society, must also exercise their voting right, working to overcome violations against the right to life. "Laws that permit abortion, euthanasia and assisted suicide are profoundly unjust, and we should work peacefully and tirelessly to oppose and change them. Because they are unjust they cannot bind citizens in conscience, be supported, acquiesced to, or recognized as valid. Our nation cannot countenance the continued existence in our society of such fundamental violations of human rights."[30]

American Catholics are in a unique position to be a positive force in working for an acceptance of the dignity of the innocent. "We encourage *all citizens,* particularly Catholics, to embrace their citizenship not merely as a duty and privilege, but as an opportunity meaningfully to participate *in building the culture of life.*"[31]

A pastoral plan prepared by the bishops focuses on four strategies by which Catholics may work to implement the gospel of life to overcome a "culture of death":

- Public information and education to deepen understanding of the sanctity of human life and the humanity of unborn children, the moral evil of intentionally killing innocent human beings—whether at the beginning of life or at its end—and the mission of the church to witness to and serve all human life.

- Pastoral care for women with problems related to pregnancy; for all who have been involved in abortion; for those who are disabled, sick and dying and their families and caregivers; for those who have lost loved ones to violent crime; and for those in prison sentenced to death.

- Public policy efforts directed to restoring legal protection to the lives of unborn children and those vulnerable to pressures to end their lives by assisted suicide, and to providing morally acceptable alternatives to abortion and assisted suicide.

- Prayer and worship directed to participation in the sacramental life of the church and in programs of communal and individual prayer, that the culture of death that surrounds us will be replaced by a culture of life and love.

Catholics are urged by the bishops to work for the promotion of pro-life efforts at every level—within their families, within the church and every other organization to which they belong. It is within the family that parents exercise their important right to be the teachers of their children in the ways of faith. "Parents are the primary educators of their children, especially in the important areas of human sexuality and the transmission of human life. They shape society toward a respect for human life by first being open to new life themselves;

then by forming their children—through personal example—with a reverence for the poor, the elderly and developing life in the womb."[32] The bishops call on all Catholics in whatever their vocation—layperson, priest, deacon, religious—to work on behalf of human life. Parents especially are called to discuss within their families the critical issues that pertain to life, to teach their children well about the sanctity of life from conception to natural death. The bishops single out in particular those who suffer from any type of disabilities and their families, since by their own testimony and example they can forcefully witness to the dignity of the human person. "Our defense of life and rejection of the culture of death requires that we acknowledge the dignity and positive contributions of our brothers and sisters with disabilities. We unequivocally oppose negative attitudes toward disability which often leads to abortion, medical rationing, and euthanasia."[33]

Reflection: People take precedence over things and structures.

Christians are called to use their prayer and worship to consecrate themselves to the values that promote respect for life. Through prayer and fasting, we attune ourselves to the promptings of the Spirit that call us to action on behalf of our Christian faith. It should be a common occurrence that our petitions at Mass reflect our desire as Christians and Americans, to become a more compassionate nation, concerned to protect the rights and dignity of each person. We pray for a change of heart—within ourselves and within the nation, that we always proclaim the protection of human life, both born and unborn.

These efforts should be coordinated at every level—
national, state, diocesan and parish. Parishes should
have a pro-life committee assisting in a special way to
make the parish a center for life, so that parishioners
will understand the needs of the most vulnerable and
the practical ways that life issues may be addressed. The
committee also should work to make sure that the annual "Respect Life "program is implemented as fully and
completely as possible.

Jesus has taught us that the greatest commandment is to
love one another as he loves us. As we seek to follow
Jesus in a profound respect for the dignity of each person, we grow in holiness and in the image of him who
created all things good.

The value of human life is being threatened today in
many ways. The dignity of life is seriously undermined
when the creation of human life is reduced to the manu-
facture of a product. The church believes that every person is precious, that people are more important than
things, and that the measure of every institution is
whether it threatens or enhances the life and dignity of
the human person.

> Eternal God
> creator and sustainer of life,
> bless us with the courage to defend all life
> from conception to natural death.
> Bless us with the strength to respect
> all peoples from east to west, from north to
>   south,
> so that we way truly follow
> the call of Jesus
> to be neighbor. . . .[34]

Reflection Questions:

1. Why is the church so concerned about the issue of the dignity of the human person?

2. Are you able to accept your own dignity as a child of God made in God's image? What hampers that realization? What enhances it? Why is self-acceptance a critical first step in working towards this issue as it surfaces in so many social justice venues?

3. What has most helped shape your present attitude towards social justice issues related to race? The death penalty? Abortion? How would you explain the Catholic church's position in regard to these issues?

4. What are the greatest threats to issues of life today? How can these threats be effectively addressed?

5. How do issues of life and social justice impact your spiritual life and development?

Chapter Three:
Call to Family, Community, and Participation

"Therefore, let us try to spread this love of Christ—above all in our own family, among our own, my husband, my wife, my children. Does my home, my community, burn in love?"

—*Mother Teresa*

Robert M. was the first of nine children and was born on March 29, 1940. After attending St. Andrew's Minor Seminary in Rochester, New York, for two years, he made a different vocational discernment and completed high school in his hometown, Ithaca, New York. After graduation he went on to receive a B.A. in accounting from Ithaca College. After wrestling with the choice of whether to study law or continue in accounting, he decided to accept an offer from the accounting firm Haskins and Sells, for which he worked for thirty-five years (under a variety of owners and name changes). Shortly after becoming a C.P.A. in 1966, he accepted a promotion to work in Brazil and he, his wife and son moved to São Paulo. In 1975 he accepted a position in Greensboro, North Carolina, in order to return to the States and to be closer to his family. His family enrolled at St. Paul the Apostle Parish, staffed by the Paulist Fathers, where Bob became active as chair of the finance committee and subsequently chair of the parish council.

In 1988 he, his wife and now three children relocated to Rochester, New York, in a move that again brought them closer to hometown Corning. In 1997 he retired from Deloitte and Touche Accounting and became immersed in various volunteer ventures for the church and other organizations. He is presently a parishioner at St. Cecilia Parish in Irondequoit, New York, where he serves as chair of the parish council and lector. He was the first chair of a reorganized finance council.

Bob organizes volunteers to assist at a men's homeless shelter where he has worked the last few years. He has also been active in United Way, a combined charitable appeal in Rochester that was founded in 1918 by local business, civic and religious leaders. This organization was founded on the principle that people in need would be best served if agencies focused their attention on delivery of services rather than gathering resources. Bob is also active in the local Rotary, another service organization of business and professional leaders that provide humanitarian service while encouraging high ethical standards in all vocations. Through the Junior Achievement program of Rotary, Bob regularly visits a fourth-grade classroom in a local public school, to assist in the development of the students' self-image and work ethic.

Bob sees a strong relationship between his spiritual life and his many activities on behalf of others. He begins each day asking God: where am I going? Where are you leading me?"
He has become much more spontaneous the last few years in planning his "to do" list, preferring to let God invite him to

new opportunities and challenges. He has also developed a perspective that sees more "God moments" in his life than hurdles, interruptions and obstacles to be overcome.

Particularly helpful to his spiritual growth has been an annual retreat experience, sometimes with a group (e.g., men from the parish at a nearby retreat house) and sometimes privately, where he spends time assessing his relationship with God. He is filled with an "attitude of gratitude" for all God has given to him and feels that "he would die, if he did not have a sense of purpose," which he believes that he receives in abundance while sharing his time and talent.

———————————

The family is identified as the basic unit of society. Jesus of Nazareth himself was born into a human family. In chapter one of Matthew's gospel, there is an extensive genealogy provided, showing how he descended from Abraham, and including mention specifically of four women in addition to Mary, the mother of Jesus. Luke also provides a genealogy, divided into four historical time periods, tracing the ancestry of the Son of God to Adam. Both the gospels of Matthew and Luke provide the immediate family background, each focusing on a different parent in the stories of Jesus' birth. In Matthew, the key parent is Joseph, who in a dream is told by an angel not to fear to take Mary as his spouse, since she has miraculously conceived by the power of the Holy Spirit (1:8–25). In Luke's recounting of the birth of Jesus, it is Mary who is told by the angel Gabriel that she will be overshadowed by the power of the Holy Spirit and will bring forth a child who will be called Jesus (1:26–38). Luke also describes the lack of lodging that results in the child being born in a manger since there was no room in the place where travelers lodged (2:6–7). The shepherds visit the child and his parents soon after his birth, after having been told of the miraculous event by the angels (2:8–18). After his birth, Jesus' parents fulfill all the legal family requirements. He is presented in the temple for the customary ritual of the law, where Simeon the prophet proclaims Jesus destiny, "a revealing light to the Gentiles, the glory of your people Israel" (2:32).

Luke presents the portrait of a family with typical family difficulties. For example, on a pilgrimage to Jerusalem, Jesus' parents fear that he is lost (2:41–52). However, it is discovered that he has remained in the city and discoursed with the religious leaders on matters sublime. "Did you not know I had to be in my Father's house?" (2:49) Jesus inquires. But he returns with his parents to Nazareth, where, Luke tells us, he was subject to them. "There he lived, quietly, we assume, with Mary and Joseph for most of his life."[1] The two evangelists show Jesus growing up in a family with loving parents: "Any person who is as whole and free as Jesus was had to have extraordinary parents. They must have loved him without manipulation, without those primitive patterns of shaming and threatening that are so common."[2]

The gospels, as they relate Jesus' later ministry, likewise contain references to his family. These allusions are not always testimonials. For example, in the Gospel of Mark (3:31–35) the family comes to see Jesus, to bring him home. Here he questions: who really comprises his family? "These are my mother and my brothers. Whoever does the will of God is brother and sister and mother to me" (3:34). In Luke's account of this same incident, Jesus states that those who hear the word of God and act upon it are his mother and brothers (8:21). Jesus emerged from a human family, which serves as a model for our own family relationships. Jesus goes on to expand the notion of family, however, to include all those who willingly accept God's will and put the Good News into practice. At times, the affirmation of the priority of the gospel over even family objections will challenge the believer. "Whoever loves father or mother, son or daughter, more than me is not worthy of me" (Mt 10:37). All loyalties—even family loyalties—must give place to loyalty to God. Jesus creates a new family paradigm, beyond the definition of bloodlines.

Reflection: The mystery of the Trinity involves the relationship of complete love among the three divine Persons—Father, Son, and Holy Spirit.

The call to live in community, be it family, church or other—builds on the loving relationship of the Godhead, Father, Son, and Spirit. The story is told of a confirmation ceremony where the presiding archbishop asked the candidates for a definition of the Holy Trinity. A fourteen-year-old girl answered very softly, "The Holy Trinity is three persons in one God." The archbishop, who was very hard of hearing, replied: "I didn't understand what you said." The young girl replied, "You are not supposed to, Archbishop. The Trinity is a mystery!"

This mystery was introduced as a feast into the church in the twelfth century by Saint Thomas Becket, archbishop of Canterbury. By the fourteenth century it was observed by the universal church. Each year preachers use the occasion of the feast to reflect on a mystery in reality beyond any human comprehension. A little girl one day brought home her report card from school. Her mother looked at it and then asked rather sternly, "I want you to explain to me why you got an 'F' in spelling." The little girl replied simply: "Words fail me!" So too for Christians, words fail them in describing a mystery that is at the heart of their faith. Another little girl, of pre-school age, was busy with her crayons, attempting to draw a likeness of her mother and father. After awhile she decided it would be easier to draw God. Her finished product was a confusing maze of squiggly lines. "Look, Mom," she said, "a picture of God!" Mother took one look and said, "I'm afraid that I can't find God in that picture." To which the little girl replied, "He's in there somewhere!" Sometimes, our understanding of the Trinitarian God, formed over many years, endless religion classes and countless sermons, can lack a precision of dogmatic formulation, but still speaks eloquently to our faith.

Pope John Paul II in *Crossing the Threshold of Hope* replies to questions posed to him by author Vittorio Messori on the occasion of the pope's fiftieth anniversary of priesthood. Originally intended to be a filmed interview, due to time constraints and the pope's schedule, the pope instead prepared written responses to the interviewer's questions. These replies were later published as an informal portrait of the thoughts of the 265th occupant of the See of Peter. The interviewer tried to ask questions ordinary people would ask if they were ever given the chance to speak to the pope. One such question concerns the existence of God; as asked by the questioner, "If God exists, why is He hiding?" Many people long for a more tangible and accessible proof of his existence. "Why does His mysterious strategy seem to be that of playing hide and seek with His creatures?"[3] John Paul responds with biblical references to people of the Hebrew Scriptures, such as Moses, and the Christian Scriptures, such as the apostles, who all struggled with the same question. Moses wanted to see God face to face but could only see his back. "When my glory passes, I will set you in the hollow of the rock and will cover you with my hand until I have passed by. Then I will remove my hand, so that you may see my back; but my face is not to be seen" (Ex 33:23). The day before Jesus' death, Philip asked him: "Show us the Father and that will be enough for us" (Jn 14:8). Jesus speaks to his special relationship: "Whoever has seen me has seen the Father. How can you say, 'Show us the Father'? Do you not believe that I am in the Father and the Father is in me?" (Jn 14:9b–10).

In a certain sense, reasons the pope, God has gone "too far" in self-disclosure. God has been revealing himself, culminating in the revelation of Jesus Christ, the Word made flesh. "Precisely because He called God His Father, because He revealed Him so openly, in Himself, He could not but elicit the impression that it was too much. . . . Man was no longer able to tolerate such closeness, and thus the protests began."[4] God, says John Paul, reveals himself in mystery. "He was not unmindful of the fact that such an unveiling would in a certain way obscure Him in the eyes of man, because man is not capable of withstanding an excess of the mystery."[5] The most central mystery of God's self-disclosure is the Trinity, the three-fold expression of divine love in Father, Son, and Holy Spirit. "It is the source of all the other mysteries of faith, the light that enlightens them."[6] It is in the name of God, as Father, Son and Holy Spirit that Christians are baptized. "Before receiving the sacrament, they respond to a three-part question when asked to confess the Father, the Son and the Spirit: 'I do.' "The faith of all Christians rests on the Trinity."[7]

---

*Reflection: As people made in
God's image, we must model
divine love.*

Although baptized individually into the Christian faith,
we are at the same time called to a life of community.
"We do not follow Jesus in isolation: we are social creatures and pilgrims who need the company of other way-
farers."[8] As we make our pilgrim way to the kingdom,
we depend upon and rely on the support of others.
"They [other disciples] provide inspiration and encouragement, even if they do not physically accompany us
on every step of the journey."[9] As we have seen, the first
and primary community is the family. "The family
exists at the heart of all societies. It is the first and most
basic community to which every person belongs. There
is nothing more fundamental to our vitality as a society
and as a Church." According to John Paul, "the future of
humanity passes by way of the family" (*On the Family*,
no. 86).[10] Like the "Prime Community," the Trinity, the
family is a relationship of love. "The story of family life
is a story about love—shared, nurtured, and sometimes
rejected for lost. In every family God is revealed uniquely and personally, for God is love and those who live in
love, live in God and God dwells in them" (cf. 1 Jn
4:16).[11] Each family knows struggles as well as joys, but
is called to be centered on the Lord Jesus. ". . . [T]he
basic vocation of every person, whether married or living a celibate life, is the same: *follow the way of love, even
as Christ loved you* (cf. Eph 5:2). The Lord issues this call
to [. . .] every family regardless of its condition or circumstances."[12] The family models the Trinitarian

relationship of the Godhead: "The Christian family is a communion of persons, a sign and image of the communion of the Father and the Son in the Holy Spirit."[13]

Through our baptism, we are united in community with God. Family life is therefore sacred, since it confirms and deepens this union. "The profound and the ordinary moments of daily life—mealtimes, workdays, vacations, expressions of love and intimacy, household chores, caring for a sick child or elderly parent, and even conflicts over things like how to celebrate holidays, discipline children, or spend money—all are the threads from which [we] can weave a pattern of holiness."[14]

Jesus promised that he would be present when believers were gathered in his name: "Where two or three are gathered in my name, there am I in their midst" (Mt 18:20). The word *church* is used to describe the people of God as they gather together, who strive to make his presence known as they follow Jesus' way of love. Family is the most basic way that the Lord calls his people. "A family is our first community and the most basic way in which the Lord gathers us, forms us, and acts in the world. The early church expressed this truth by calling the Christian family *a domestic church or church of the home.*"[15] This domestic church cannot stand alone. It must be united and supported by parishes and other communities that are a part of the larger church. However, each family shares in the mission of the whole church. This is accomplished when:

- belief in God is nurtured within the family;

- love for one another in the family is nurtured;

- appropriate intimacy is fostered, with each member of the family sharing with the whole family—both good and bad qualities—and is accepted by the entire family;

- the family evangelizes, publicly professing the faith and setting an example of Christian living;

- parents educate their children, helping them to acquire values necessary for Christian living;

- families pray together, thanking God for blessings and seeking help and guidance in time of need;

- members of the family serve one another, sacrificing one's personal wants and needs for the sake of someone else;

- family members seek forgiveness for wrongs that have been committed, letting go of old hurts and grudges;

- life is celebrated in both sadness and joy—birthdays and deaths, holidays and holy days;

- strangers are welcomed in imitation of the gospel command to see Christ in others and to offer comfort and compassion;

- justice is proclaimed and practiced within the community, and the rights of others are treated with respect;

- life is affirmed as a precious gift from God;

- vocations to ministry are encouraged and fostered.[16]

To develop as a domestic church is not easy. At times such a vocation can be overwhelming. "Perhaps they consider their family too 'broken' to be used for the Lord's purpose. But, remember, a family is holy not because it is perfect, but because God's grace is at work in it, helping it to set out anew everyday on the way of love."[17]

> The unique role of each Person of the Trinity can be seen reflected in the Christian family. For example, the procreation and education of children reflects the Father's work of creation. The family likewise is called to partake in the prayer and sacrifice of Christ (see *C.C.C.*, no. 2205). The family becomes a "privileged community," with relationships that contain an "affinity of feelings, affections and interests" which arise from the members' respect for one another (see *C.C.C.*, no. 2206).

Reflection: The human person is not only sacred, but also social.

The vocation of the human being in this life is to know God, the creator, and to be transformed into the likeness of the Son, Jesus Christ (cf. *C.C.C.*, no. 1877). Every person who comes into the world is called to the same end, i.e., union with God. But this adventure in faith takes place not in solitary fashion, but within the context of community, in society. As taught in the Second Vatican Council document, *The Church in the Modern World (Gaudium et Spes)*, "Man's social nature makes it evident that the progress of the human person and the advance of society itself hinge on each other. For the beginning, the subject and the goal of all social institutions is and must be the human person, which for its part and by its very nature stands completely in need of social life."[18] There exist mutual ties and dependencies which involve us every day in a variety of associations and organizations. Interaction with society is not something added on to the nature of the human being. "Through the exchange with others, mutual service and dialogue with his brethren, man develops his potential; he thus responds to his vocation."[19] It is within society that the person comes to know him or herself, the unique potential and the individual talents that must be developed for the sake of the common good. "This development, which is called socialization, while certainly not without its dangers, brings with it many advantages with respect to consolidating and increasing the qualities of the human person, and safeguarding his rights."[20]

Besides the family, each person also participates in that community known as the state, the natural development and need of peoples to associate together to accomplish goals and objectives which they cannot achieve alone. However, as reminded by the Second Vatican Council, "the human person . . . is and ought to be the principle, the subject, and the object of every social organization" (*The Church in the Modern World*, no. 25, §1).

> Catholicism does not call us to abandon the world, but to help shape it. This does not mean leaving worldly tasks and responsibilities, but transforming them. Catholics are everywhere in this society. We are corporate executives and migrant workers, senators and welfare recipients, university presidents and day care workers, tradesmen and farmers, office and factory workers, union leaders and small

business owners. Our entire community of
faith must help Catholics to be instruments
of God's grace and creative power in business and politics, factories and offices, in
homes and schools and in all the events of
daily life.[21]

Reflection: We realize our digni-
ty and rights in relationship
with others, in community.

In every society there must necessarily exist authority
that assures that the human community is well ordered
and that its institutions are properly preserved. Certain
people must be selected to make sure that laws are
made and orders are given for proper governance. The
Christian faith teaches that the authority required by the
moral order comes from God: "Let every person be subject to the governing authorities; for there is no authority except from God, and those authorities that exist
have been instituted by God. Therefore whoever resists
authority resists what God has appointed, and those
who resist will incur judgment" (Rom 13:1–2 NRSV; cf. 1
Pt 2:13–17). Such authority must act for the common
good, which in turn is defined in reference to the human
person. By common good is meant "the sum total of
social conditions which allow people, either as a group
or as individuals to reach their fulfillment more fully
and more easily" (*The Church in the Modern World*, no.
26). The common good presupposes a certain respect for
the person and respect for the inalienable and fundamental rights of the human person.

"Our political choices should not reflect simply our own
interests, partisan preferences or ideological agendas,
but should be shaped by the principles of our faith and

our commitment to justice, especially to the weak and vulnerable."[22] There are a variety of issues perennially facing the American electorate that demand a Christian response: "The voices and votes of lay Catholics are needed to shape a society with greater respect for human life, economic and environmental justice, cultural diversity and global solidarity."[23]

Reflection: The family has major contributions to make in addressing questions of social justice.

In the family, parents provide an environment where offspring learn the virtues of humanity, where the child learns what it means to be a "human person." Hopefully the child assimilates a proclivity for sharing the Christian values learned at home. The aim of Christian education is to develop a Christian who responsibly and publicly shows Christian commitment to causes that require faith put into action. As Pope Paul VI stated in *On The Development of Peoples (Populorum Progressio)*: ". . . [I]t belongs to the [laity], without waiting passively for orders and directives, to take the initiative freely and to infuse a Christian spirit into the mentality, customs, laws and structures of the community in which they live."[24] This commitment is perhaps most needed in social justice issues that pertain to life. As Pope John Paul II has frequently commented, there are many today who refuse to even consider the possibility of bringing new life into the world, so concerned are they with the things of this world. People can think of children as: "things"—something to be had or not had, depending on the particular whim of the moment.

John Paul sees the family as the "sanctuary of life," the place in which life—the gift of God—can be properly welcomed and protected against the many attacks to which it is exposed, and can develop in accordance with what constitutes authentic human growth. Consequently, the "role of the family in building a culture of life is *decisive and irreplaceable.*"[25] He sees a certain sacral quality, that place where the human being, the gift of life, the gift from God—can be welcomed and protected against the forces of the world that could bring it harm. "Within the 'people of life and the people for life,' *the family has a decisive responsibility.* This responsibility flows from its very nature as a community of life and love, founded upon marriage, and from its mission to 'guard, reveal and communicate love.'"[26]

It is sad that especially in contemporary society, the individual is seen more as a consumer of goods. "It is a strict duty of justice and truth not to allow fundamental human needs to remain unsatisfied, and not to allow those burdened by such needs to perish. It is also necessary to help these needy people to acquire expertise, to enter the circle of exchange, and to develop their skills in order to make the best use of their capacities and resources."[27] The teachings of the church concerning the social gospel seek to elevate the human person. It is in the family that this fundamental concept is first taught and thoroughly appreciated.

The Dogmatic Constitution on the Church, (*Lumen Gentium*), addresses the need for laity to be immersed in the works of justice. "The laity, by their very vocation seek the kingdom of God by engaging in temporal affairs and by ordering them to the plan of God. They live in the world, that is, in each and in all the secular professions and occupations . . . they can work for the sanctification of the world from within, in the manner of leaven."[28]

Unfortunately, many Christians divide their life between a perceived "secular vocation" and "Christian" vocation, compartmentalizing their Christianity to church attendance and/or church committee work and activities. "The implication is not that Christians are terribly immoral on the job or around the community. It is rather, that Christians are not very conscious that their workaday life is a primary expression of their response to God, that work itself puts holiness into life."[29] Therefore, claims William Droel, such a dichotomy (work world vs. church time) veers from the original intention of the Council: ". . . [V]atican II, a watershed in modern Christianity, signaled a major shift in the relationship between faith and wider world of work, politics, art, education, and civic life. Unlike a sect that tries to maintain a safe distance (and thus its purity) from the established centers of culture, commerce and industry, Vatican II envisioned a community of Christians at the center of human enterprise."[30]

Now more than ever, the family must impact the society in which it finds itself with strong Christian values, which begin in the home. "The family is a mediating structure between the individual and mega-institutions. It both forms a person to carry values into the world and buffers the individual from impersonal forces in that world."[31] Appreciating the value, beauty and dignity of the person, the older members of society as well as the young, a vision is developed within the society that reverences the beauty of each of God's creations. Each person makes good and prudent choices at the family, social and international level, on the basis of a correct scale of values. As Pope John Paul II has said, these choices will be based on "being" over "having."

Reflection: The family is where we learn and act on our values.

Jesus often told parables that used family images. Perhaps the most vivid use is the familiar story of the two brothers, one of which demands an early disposition of his share of his inheritance (Lk 15:11–32). Often called the story of the "Prodigal Son," it is better entitled the story of the "Merciful Father." There takes place an unfolding realization by the son, after squandering all of his money, that he has not chosen wisely and should return to his father, so he decides to return home. The father, after searching the highways in expectant hope that his son might return, runs to embrace the wayward son. The son is heartily welcomed home with great joy by the father—with a banquet and a fatted calf—much to the dismay of a jealous older brother. In typical sibling rivalry, the older son complains to the father. He has been faithful and dutiful with no apparent appreciation shown by the father for his loyalty. The father reaffirms his love—"all that I have is yours"—but we must rejoice because he who was lost is now found.

It is in just such give and take within the family that great moral lessons are learned and the gospel takes root in the lives of parents and children. The opportunity for building faith values in a family to a great extent depends on families being together for extended periods of time—not easily accomplished in today's hectic society. "The relationship between the culture and family life is something like a river on which family life sometimes glides with positive cultural currents, but at other times must row harder against these currents."[32] It is in the family where the basic teachings about the gospel are taught, learned and practiced. It is also the concern of the church that governments be responsible in reinforcing the importance of the family, assuring that each family is properly protected, supported and encouraged.

> *Reflection: We have the right
> and the responsibility to partici-
> pate in and contribute to the
> broader communities in society.*

According to the U.S. bishops, the principle of participation in society's structures is a corollary to the natural
impulse to form family and subsequently to form community. In the U.S. bishops' *Economic Justice for All:
Pastoral Letter on Catholic Social Teaching and the U.S.
Economy*, they forcefully acknowledged that poverty
encompasses "more than a lack of material resources.
Poverty denies full participation in the life of the community and impedes the ability to influence decisions
impacting one's life."[33] In addressing the issue of poverty within society, the government not only works to
improve on possible inequities within the economic system, but at the same time fosters participation by all
members in the body politic.

> *Reflection: A central test of politi-
> cal, legal, and economic institu-
> tions is what they do to people,
> what they do for people, and how
> people participate in them.*

The baptismal vocation, strengthened in confirmation,
propels the Christian to be the leaven in society, perme-
ating the world with Christian values. Pope John Paul
was to return to this same responsibility in his encyclical
Centesimus Annus: "It is a strict duty of justice and truth
not to allow fundamental human needs to remain unsatisfied, and not to allow those burdened by such needs to

perish. It is also necessary to help those needy people to acquire expertise, to enter the circle of exchange, and to develop their skills in order to make the best use of their capacities and resources" (no. 34). Institutions and governments are made up of individuals called to work together for the common good, promoting the fundamental rights of each person.

> Embracing Father,
> You grace each of us with equal measure
>   in your love.
> Let us learn to love our neighbors more
>   deeply,
> so that we can create
> peaceful and just communities.
> Inspire us to use our creative energies
> to build the structures we need
> to overcome the obstacles
> of intolerance and indifference.
> May Jesus provide us the example needed
>   and send the Spirit to warm our hearts
>   for the journey.
> Amen.[34]

Reflection Questions:

1. What is the role of the family in developing a consciousness of social issues/social justice?

2. How can parents best demonstrate gospel values to their children?

3. What are the biggest challenges to families in living the Gospel today?

4. How may the church best address new forms of family life?

5. How could you best advocate for the nurturing of strong gospel values in family life within your own local community?

6. How can we best enhance and celebrate the gifts of the elderly among us?

Chapter Four:
Rights and Responsibilities of the Human Person

"The Gospel is the fullest confirmation of
the role of human rights."
— *Pope John Paul II*

*Beth L. was born in Gasport, New York, a village of about
1,300 with longtime ties to vegetable farming, named after
local springs that emitted flammable gas, in the southern tier
of New York State. After attending the local public grammar
and high school, she enrolled at Nazareth College, a school of
the liberal arts near Rochester, New York, where she obtained
her B.A. in English. After completing her degree (1964) she
entered the Sisters of St. Joseph, a religious congregation
founded in the mid-1600s in LePuy, France. Forced under-
ground by the French Revolution, the order emerged in Lyon,
France in 1807, dedicated to practicing "all the spiritual and
corporal works of mercy of which woman is capable and which
will most benefit the . . . neighbor."*

*Sr. Beth enrolled in theological studies at the University of
Notre Dame and after graduation began teaching theology at
a high school operated by her community. For several years
she served on the leadership team for her congregation,
including two terms as superior general. For the last several
years she has been active in community organizing in the
Rochester metropolitan area, including the creation of the
Progressive Neighborhood Federal Credit Union, an effort to
help low-income residents gain access to credit and become
responsible managers of their finances. Founded with only
$10,000 in start-up money collected by Sr. Beth, the credit
union now totals assets of over $2.4 million dollars. Her
efforts have also been instrumental in bridging economic
divides by her work in Partners for Food and the Community
Microenterprise Center, which attempts to broaden access to
food, financial services and economic opportunity. She has
recently completed her term as president of the Greater
Rochester Community of Churches, an ecumenical organization directed towards joint outreach programs.*

*She traces her compassionate concern for those deprived to her
father, who owned a shoe store in Gasport. There she observed
his respect for all his clientele, including the indigent. A religious sister who early on noticed her preference for the
"underdog" prophesied that Sr. Beth would be attracted to
working with "the simple, the weak and the good." She has
been greatly influenced by the charism of her community, an
element of which is to "walk in any world"—the rich and the
poor—and to always be "one with the people." Personal
prayer and the eucharist have become central to her spirituality, where she is "washed by the words" of Scripture.*

There is perhaps nothing that resonates within
Americans more than the protection of "rights." The
United States was founded on the principle that basic

human rights exist. As the American Declaration of Independence states: "We hold these truths to be self-evident, that all men are created equal, that they are endowed by their creator with certain unalienable Rights, that among these among these are Life, Liberty and the pursuit of Happiness,—That to secure these rights, Governments are instituted among Men, deriving their just power from the consent of the governed. . . ." An emphasis upon rights has also been, as well, a part of Catholic social teaching. Here, the basis for the rights that come to each person is the dignity of the person, made in the image of God.

One of the biggest challenges to the church today is the carry over of our Christian social teaching about rights into the "marketplace":

> How do we connect worship on Sunday to work on Monday? How is the Gospel proclaimed not only in the pulpits of our parishes, but also in the everyday lives of Catholic people? How does the church gathered on the Sabbath act as the People of God scattered and active every day of the week? How can we best carry the values of our faith into family life, the market place and the public square? How do we love our neighbor, pursue peace and seek justice in everyday choices and commitments?[1]

The response to the questions raised by the bishops is critical, since the answers will demonstrate how effectively the Catholic community can engage the larger society concerning issues of human rights. There are many venues where the Christian can engage in the ongoing struggle to promote rights' values. "The

Catholic social mission is also carried forward by believers who join unions, neighborhood organizations, business groups, civic associations, the pro-life movement, groups working for justice, or environmental, civil rights or peace groups. It is advanced by Christians who stand up for the values of the Gospel."[2] As reminded by *The Dogmatic Constitution on the Church*, the role of the laity in this regard is critical: "The laity, by their very vocation, seek the kingdom of God by engaging in temporal affairs and by ordering them to the plan of God. They live in the world, that is, in each and in all the secular professions and occupations. . . . They can work for the sanctification of the world from within, in the manner of leaven" (no. 11). This ongoing ministry takes place daily and often without much fanfare. "This mission is the task of countless Christians living their faith without much fanfare or recognition, who are quietly building a better society by their choices and actions day by day."[3] Unfortunately the mission is often not appreciated or understood by the laity themselves. ". . . Christians are not very conscious that their workaday life is a primary expression of their response to God, that work itself puts holiness into life. From another angle, Christians do not normally pray and worship in a way that allows their work, family and community life to shape and challenge that prayer."[4] But the impact of such activism cannot and should not be minimalized. It is at the core of the involvement called upon by the Second Vatican Council:

> The *sine qua non* of the Vatican II understanding of the church-in-the-world is a refurbished notion of the laity. In fact, Vatican II collapses without a lay model. According to Vatican II, Christians live their faith by sustaining and improving

familial, cultural, economic, political, and
social institutions. The Christian vocation
is lived by attending office meetings, by
participating in a local union, by agitating
for improved delivery of services at the
college, hospital or agency, and by hundreds of other daily activities. As insiders
to society, Christians are called to [be] salt
and light in their professions, occupations,
and states of life.[5]

Thankfully, many Christians are making a significant
impact on their communities each day. "They protect
human life, defend those who are poor, seek the common good, work for peace, and promote human dignity."[6] Working on behalf of the rights of others is not
always welcomed. "Working for justice in everyday life
is not easy. There are complex and sometimes difficult
challenges encountered by women and men as they try
to live their faith in the world. We applaud the efforts of
all Catholics to live the Gospel by pursuing justice and
peace in their everyday choices and commitments."[7]

Reflection: Flowing from our
God-given dignity, each
person has basic rights and
responsibilities.

Pope John XXIII in his encyclical of 1963, *Pacem in Terris*
(Peace on Earth) addressed issues of world peace beginning with a discussion of the presence of order within
society and between nations. He used principles of natural law as his premise. "The progress of learning and
the inventions of technology clearly show that, both in
living things and in the forces of nature, an astonishing
order reigns, and they also bear witness to the greatness

of man, who can understand that order and create suitable instruments to harness those forces of nature and use them to his benefit."[8] He went on to an approach to peace, based on the natural order found in the hearts of people. "But the Creator of the world has imprinted in man's heart an order which his conscience reveals to him and enjoins him to obey: *This shows that the obligations of the law are written in their hearts; their conscience utters its own testimony* (Rom 2:15)."[9]

As each person looks into his or her heart and reflects on God's designs, there is an unmistakable conclusion that God's imprint is found in the human person. Listening to their heart, people come to know how they should interact with others and, even on a larger scale, how nations should deal with other nations. According to John XXIII the natural law disposes towards an understanding of a well-ordered society built on the respect for the dignity of the human person.

> Any human society, if it is to be well-ordered and productive, must lay down as a foundation this principle, namely, that every human being is a person, that is, his nature is endowed with intelligence and free will. Indeed, precisely because he is a person he has rights and obligations flowing directly and simultaneously from his very nature. And as these rights and obligations are universal and inviolable so they cannot in any way be surrendered.[10]

Beginning with the dignity of the person, John XXIII enumerates several rights, including standards of living, moral and cultural values, worship according to one's conscience, choosing freely one's state of life, economic rights, of meeting and association, to emigrate and to immigrate, and political rights.[11]

Included in "political rights" is the right to take an active part in public affairs and to participate in society. *The Catechism of the Catholic Church* speaks of this participation as the voluntary and generous engagement of a person in social interchange (no. 1913), which takes place first of all through the assumption of personal responsibility for the care and education of one's family and by conscientious work (no. 1914). The Christian, in addition, is called to participation in the public life of the society. The church encourages and praises those countries who foster such participation: "One must pay tribute to those nations whose systems permit the largest possible number of the citizens to take part in public life in a climate of genuine freedom."[12] "The principle of common good points to the concern Christians should have for the cooperative behavior and the communal structures that produce good things like clean air, healthy surroundings, available healthcare, accountable politics, fair laws, meaningful jobs, world peace, and more."[13] As author William Droel goes on to explain, the concept of the common good includes things and activities that we might consider within the realm of the private sector. "Actually, the concept of common good also reminds people that even so-called private goods cannot be obtained without the cooperation of hundreds of people routinely acting through well-functioning markets, companies, organizations, and other institutions."[14]

The church is also aware that in any society, working actively on behalf of the common good requires ongoing conversion. "Fraud and other subterfuges, by which some people evade the constraints of the law and the prescriptions of societal obligations, must be firmly condemned because they are incompatible with the requirements of justice."[15]

It is important that care be taken to promote institutions that improve the conditions of human life. ". . . [T]he common good does not believe that an unfettered market and individual calculus will eventually produce the best results for all. Instead, the common good pictures society like an organism with interdependent parts. While tradeoffs have to be constantly made, the common good warns that each piece of society, each piece of a family, each sector of a city is priceless."[16]

Sometimes, leaders in a society with a democratically-elected government are perceived as furthering their own ambitions, acquiring personal benefits at the expense of those who elected them to office. It is important that those who are given the responsibility to exercise authority on behalf of the commonwealth must be firmly committed to strengthening the values of society by encouraging all members to service for the common good. "One is entitled to think that the future of humanity is in the hands of those who are capable of providing the generations to come with reasons for life and optimism."[17] The church prods society to an understanding of leadership in terms of service. "Whoever would be great among you must be your servant" (Mt 20:26). Droel speaks of "Incarnational Christians . . . committed to transforming our messy world and finding holiness in so doing."[18] Such Christians accept leadership in the community but with a different twist. They are able to see the potential for conversion within the daily grind of civic interactions: "Incarnational Christians are sensitive to the sacred potential in what appears to be mundane human experience in their work, leisure and neighborliness, worship, acts of citizenship, preaching, catechesis, and social action. Incarnational Christians know that embedded in the ordinary lies the extraordinary, the miraculous, the salvific, the holy."[19] Such Christians embrace the call to leadership, not waiting to be empowered, but acknowledging their giftedness:

> Incarnational Christians are eager to gather with like-minded Christians and others to transform the world. Without hesitation, each baptized person must take the initiative. Mature Christian women and men do not wait for programs emanating from a rectory or diocesan agency in order to shoulder their responsibility in the world. Today's Incarnational Christians gladly cooperate with priests, religious, and other church employees in advancing the faith in the home, the neighborhood, and the marketplace.[20]

Such leaders will commit themselves to work for the dignity of persons, based on natural law principles of respect for the individual. "Political authorities are obliged to respect the fundamental rights of the human person. They will dispense justice humanely by respecting the rights of everyone, especially of families and the disadvantaged."[21] The bishops, in their statement "Living the Gospel of Life: A Challenge to American Catholics," reflected on the mission given to Catholics who serve in political offices, to protect and preserve the right to life in their deliberations.

> . . . [S]ome Catholic elected officials have adopted the argument that, while they personally oppose evils like abortion, they cannot force their religious views onto the wider society. This is seriously mistaken in several counts. First, regarding abortion, the point when human life begins is not a

religious belief but a scientific fact—a fact on which there is clear agreement even among leading abortion advocates. Second, the sanctity of human life is not merely Catholic doctrine but part of humanity's global ethical heritage, and our nation's founding principle. Finally, democracy is not served by silence. Most Americans would recognize the contradiction in the statement, 'while I am personally opposed to slavery or racism or sexism, I cannot force my personal view on the rest of society.'[22]

So, too, Catholic citizens within a democratic state are called to participate in the responsibilities of citizenry from a specifically Christian moral perspective. "Democracy is not a substitute for morality, nor a panacea for immorality. Its value stands—or falls—with the values which it embodies and promotes."[23] American Catholics have long sought to be accepted by American society. This has its pitfalls. "But in assimilating, we have too often been digested. We have been changed by our culture too much, and we have changed it not enough."[24]

Although called to cooperate with those who legitimately exercise civil authority, the citizen is sometimes confronted with the moral test: compliance with actions or directives that are contrary to the demands of the moral order, to the fundamental rights of persons or to the teachings of the Gospel. "Refusing obedience to civil authorities, when their demands are contrary to those of an upright conscience, finds its justification in the distinction between serving God and serving the political community: 'Render to Caesar the things that are Caesar's, and to God the things that are God's.'"[25]

The church has the obligation and right to impact the state with its vision of the human person. "The Church invites political authorities to measure their judgments and decisions against this inspired truth about God and man."[26] The church must be careful not to identify itself with any particular government or political community, lest it jeopardize its salvific mission. This leaves the church free "to pass moral judgments even in matters related to politics, whenever the fundamental rights of man or the salvation of souls require it. The means, the only means, she may use are those which are in accord with the Gospel and the welfare of all . . . [people] according to the diversity of time and circumstances."[27]

The call of the Gospel life is to *activity* on behalf of the Good News. "Be doers of the word, and not merely hearers. . . . Faith by itself, if it has no works, is dead" (Jas 1:22, 2:17 NRSV). Jesus sends Christians forth "to make disciples of all nations" (Mt 28:19). "Life in Christ is a life of active witness. It demands moral leadership. Each and every person baptized in the truth of the Catholic faith is a member of the 'people of life' sent by God to evangelize the world."[28]

Reflection: People have a fundamental right to life and to those things that make life truly human: food, clothing, housing, health care, education, security, social services, and employment.

Society has a right and obligation to help in the attainment of living conditions that allow its citizens to grow and reach maturity, including food and clothing, housing, health care, basic education, employment and social assistance (see *C.C.C.*, no. 2288). The social concern of the church is always directed toward the authentic development of the person and society. Several popes, including John Paul II, have pointed to the ever widening gap between the areas of the developed North and the developing South. "The abundance of goods and services available in some parts of the world, particularly in the developed North, is matched in the South by an unacceptable delay, and it is precisely in this geopolitical area that the major part of the human race lives."[29] The pope is troubled by the continuing disparity: "Looking at all the various sectors—the production and distribution of foodstuffs, hygiene, health and housing, availability of drinking water, working conditions (especially for women), life expectancy and other economic and social indicators—the general picture is a disappointing one, both considered in itself and in relation to the corresponding data of the more developed countries. The word 'gap' returns spontaneously to mind."[30] The gap is easily seen:

> As we observe the various parts of the world separated by this widening gap, and note that each of these parts seems to follow its own path with its own achievements, we can understand the current usage which speaks of different worlds within our one world: The First World, the Second World, the Third World and at times the Fourth World. Such expressions, which obviously do not claim to classify exhaustively all countries, are significant: they are a sign of a widespread sense that the unity of the world, that is, the unity of the human race, is seriously compromised.[31]

Since the church is a "sign and an instrument" of the unity of the whole human race, it cannot remain indifferent.[32] This is not solely the responsibility of private institutions. It is a major task of government. "This does not mean that government has the primary or exclusive role, but it does have a positive moral responsibility in safeguarding human rights and ensuring that the minimum conditions of human dignity are met for all. In a democracy, government is a means by which we can act together to protect what is important to us and to promote our common values."[33] Pope John XXIII, in his encyclical *Pacem in Terris,* was quite clear in affirming the basis of peace in the ability and willingness of a society to provide the environment for order within society—an order that is placed in society by God. Order between and among persons is fostered by the common recognition of rights and obligations. Such "natural rights" include the right to a good reputation, freedom in searching for truth and expressing and communicating opinions, the pursuit of art within the limits laid down by the moral order and common good. There is as well the right to be informed truthfully about public events. But the natural law also provides for the right to share in the benefits of culture and basic education, the right to worship as one's conscience dictates and to practice one's religion publicly and privately.

Reflection: Corresponding to these rights are duties and responsibilities—to one another, to our families, and to the larger society—to respect the rights of others and to work for the common good.

99

Through the years, the church has taught the need to foster and develop various social rights. She realizes that such efforts can result in a transformation and even (re)awakening of a sense of the transcendent within society itself.

> When the relations of human society are expressed in terms of rights and duties, men [and women] become conscious of spiritual values . . . they are brought to a better knowledge of the true God Who is personal and transcendent, and thus they make the ties that bind them to God the solid foundation and supreme criterion of their lives, both of that life which they live interiorly in the depths of their own souls and of that in which they are united to other men [and women] in society.[34]

The challenge for Christians concerning the common good in today's society is most clearly seen in the area of the economy. The gospels have much to say to us about even modern economics, with a wisdom that does not grow old or outmoded. One needs look no further than the Beatitudes, which declare as holy people and circumstances not normally associated with holiness such as the "poor in spirit": "When we exercise our option to view economics under the banner of the Beatitudes, we gradually rid ourselves of blindness. We begin to realize how frequently and how easily economic success and power are leagued with 'unjust mammon' with sinful economic structures and degrading exploitation and relationships."[35]

The United States is a country that treasures initiative and free enterprise. Americans are encouraged to seek their dreams and for many it is the prosperous life. But can this be considered a "right"? What are the obligations owed by those who "have" to those who "have not?" The American bishops in 1986, after much consultation, including a variety of economic specialists, issued a pastoral letter on the economy which used principles of Catholic social teaching to examine issues of the American economy. They also recognized that the U.S. plays a major role in the interdependent global economy, so that the issues of economic justice have an impact beyond the national boundaries. "The global economy is made up of national economies of industrialized nations of the North and the developing countries of the South, together with the network of economic relations that link them. It constitutes the framework in which the solidarity we seek on a national level finds its international expression."[36] The bishops made clear that teachings of the church concerning social justice impact many issues and relationships in the economic sector. Traditional Catholic teaching on this global interdependence emphasizes the dignity of the human person, the unity of the human family, the universally beneficial purpose of the goods of the earth, the need to pursue the international common good, as well as the good of each nation, and the imperative of distributive justice."[37] The bishops in their letter warned that measures were needed to promote social teachings in the relations of the U.S. with the Third World. "Unless conscious steps are taken toward protecting human dignity and fostering human solidarity in these relationships, we can look forward to increased conflict and inequity, threatening the fragile economies of relatively poor nations far more than our relatively strong one."[38] As an illustration, the bishops point to how disadvantaged large numbers of people are in this interdependent world: "Half the world's people, nearly two and a half billion, live in countries where the annual per capita income is $400 or less. At least 800 million people in those countries live in absolute poverty, 'beneath any rational definition of human decency.'"[39] The bishops go on to discuss the issue of hunger: "Nearly half a billion are chronically hungry, despite abundant harvests world-wide."[40] The bishops are remarkably blunt in placing blame for such inequities: "No aggregate of individual examples could portray adequately the appalling inequities within those desperately poor countries and between them and our own. And their misery is not the inevitable result of the march of history or of the intrinsic nature of particular cultures, but of human decisions and human institutions."[41]

Such issues cannot be removed from consideration of domestic policy in an interdependent and global economy. "The notion of interdependence erases the fading line between domestic and foreign policy. Many foreign policy decisions (for example, on trade, investment, and immigration) have direct and substantial impact on domestic constituencies in the United States. Similarly, many decisions thought of as domestic (for example, on farm policy, interest rates, the federal budget, or the deficit) have important consequences for other countries."[42] Such observations lead inescapably to the conclusion that Christians must continue to reflect on the linkage of domestic and foreign issues to the Gospel and ask new and reformatted moral questions.

Other domestic issues that directly challenge Americans in terms of the Gospel of Jesus and American economic policies must also be faced. For example, the promise of the American dream for many American remains unfulfilled. "When citizens are under the oppression of a public authority which oversteps its competence, they should still not refuse to give or to do what is objectively demanded of them by the common good; but it is legitimate for them to defend their own rights and those of their fellow citizens against the abuse of the authority within the limits of the natural law and the Law of the Gospel."[43]

Jesus' ministry extended an invitation to holiness to all people. Such an invitation, when accepted sincerely, can result in a re-prioritization of values. As moral theologian Bernard Häring reminds us: "We need to be leaders in the flight from all complicity with greed and from the reckless striving for wealth and economic power that is so detrimental to so many people. Our flight, however, must not constitute a betrayal of our mission to be 'the salt of the earth,' and 'salt' also to socioeconomic life."[44] The bishops remind us that we are called as Christians to make a fundamental option for the poor, to evaluate our economic activity from the perspective of the poor and the powerless, making sure that everyone has the opportunity to participate in the community. The bishops insist that a new order be established that permits and guarantees respect for the human dignity of each person as the premise and principle of participation.

An important goal of the U. S. bishops has been full employment. Recognizing that employment exists as a protection of freedom for all to participate in the economic life of the country, work becomes central to the well being and freedom of people. The burden of full employment falls on everyone—from the government official, to the general public. Government economic policies, they insist, must work towards steady economic growth that will assure full employment.

One of the greatest scourges to afflict society, including America, is widespread poverty. Most disturbing is the number of children who are affected. As the bishops indicate, it is truly disheartening to know that there are many poor families with children who receive no government assistance, have no health insurance, and who are unable to pay any medical bills. The bishops also note that many racial minorities experience the brunt of the problems associated with poverty. They would agree that great strides have been made to overcome racial discrimination in the country over the last several years. But unfortunately, the effects of prior discrimination and its continued existence today still exclude a large number of people from the mainstream of American life.

There is inequality in the distribution of wealth in the United States today. "For many people, economic activity is governed exclusively by motives of material success, efficiency, wealth and power . . . many who call themselves Christian have followed this reasoning."[45] As Pope John Paul II states: "Those who are more influential because they have a greater share of goods and economic services, should feel responsible for the weaker and be ready to share with them all they possess. Those who are weaker, for their part . . . should not adopt a purely *passive* attitude or one that is *destructive* of the social fabric, but while claiming their legitimate rights, should do what they can for the good of all. The intermediate groups, in their turn, should not selfishly insist on their particular interests, but respect the interests of others."[46] This is where a moral vision is needed, would insist the bishops. Of primary concern must be the priority of meeting the basic needs of the poor. The focus must not be solely in providing financial assistance when needed. Rather, the true focus must be helping people to take control of their own lives and destiny. This concern must extend globally, since all peoples are entitled to participate in the global economy.

Perhaps most disturbing in the bishops' critique of the U.S. economy was the lack of effective participation of all people in the economic life of the community, a situation which when purposefully intended by a person, people or government, can result in social sin. Their goal, in writing such a pastoral letter was to point to a new order, an order which when created, would guarantee the minimum conditions of human dignity in the economic sphere for every person. The bishops have reminded us that all members of the Christian community are called to a discernment of the hurts and opportunities of the world around them, in order to respond to the pressing needs and thus build up a more just society.

> God of peace,
> give us the courage
> to be reconciled with our neighbors, our
>   enemies.
> Give us the vision
> to truly see what it means
> to be a Christian
> so that peace and justice
> may rule in our world. Amen.[47]

Reflection Questions:

1. Why is the church involved in the protection of human rights?

2. What issues in the field of human rights are particularly important in today's world?

3. What are effective ways that the church can use to promote education of human rights?

4. How can a better appreciation of rights and the dignity of the human person help in my own personal spiritual development?

5. Pope John Paul II has said that the "teaching and spreading of her social doctrine are part of the church's evangelizing mission" (*Sollicitudo Rei Socialis*, no. 41). How may I become better equipped to participate in the evangelizing mission of the church?

Chapter Five:
Option for and With the Poor and Vulnerable

Only the poor,
the hungry,
those who need someone to come on their
behalf,
   will have that someone.
That someone is God,
   Emmanuel,
   God with us.
Without poverty of spirit
   there can be no abundance of God. . . .
                 —*Oscar Romero*

Sr. Grace M. has been involved in work for the underprivileged and unrepresented for over forty years. As a teenager living in Corning, New York, after her twin brother announced upon graduation from high school that he would be studying for the priesthood, filled with sibling rivalry she announced that she would become a nun. However that vocation would not be realized for two years. After her second year of college, she entered the Sisters of Mercy in Rochester, New York, and prepared for a life of what she thought would be discipline, semi-cloister and teaching.

The decision to join a particular congregation was largely influenced by her grammar school education at St. Mary's School in where the Sisters of Mercy taught. When she was considering a religious order her pastor, whom she consulted, strongly encouraged her to enter this community that served the parish, although Grace had a certain longing for foreign mission work. But after entering and making her novitiate she became enamored with the life of the foundress, Catherine McAuley (b. 1778), daughter of a prosperous Catholic family in Ireland. Learning from her father at a young age to have compassion for the poor, Catherine transformed his legacy (spiritual and financial) into a house in Dublin, Ireland, where she and similarly minded women could take in home-less women and provide care and education for them and their children. Before long the community was canonically erected as a religious institute (1831), as the "Sisters of Mercy." This order now serves in more than twenty-five countries of the world.

After profession as a sister, Grace's first years, like most mem-bers of this congregation, were spent in teaching in Catholic grammar schools in the Diocese of Rochester. A turning point came in her life when she was assigned in the early 1960s to teach in an inner-city school, Our Lady of Mount Carmel. She became aware that many of the learning difficulties that she encountered in the classroom could be directly traced to home environment issues — poor housing, improper nutrition, etc. She started visiting the homes of all her students and began tutoring parents in, among many things, good hygiene practice, as well as basic educational subjects. She noted how, unlike their counterparts in the suburbs where she had also taught, her inner-city students were ecstatic over seeing their homework and class projects displayed, now in a bright and lively classroom setting.

When Bishop Fulton Sheen came to Rochester as bishop (1966) he expressed an interest in outreach to the inner city and appointed a priest as vicar for urban ministry. The local religious congregations were asked to provide sisters for this developing ministry. Sr. Grace was appointed to the new office and would spend the rest of her ministry actively advocating on behalf of the poor and voiceless in a variety of assignments and venues. She currently operates the House of Mercy which she founded, an emergency resource center in Rochester's inner city, providing advocacy, counseling, education and faith building, with over 4,000 weekly clients. The House of Mercy is rooted "in the life of Jesus Christ and his special love for the poor." Sr. Grace animates the spirit of the house with her own spirituality rooted in the Scriptures, especially the Gospels and the prophets. She says that she could not do what she does, "without daily reflecting on the life of Jesus, reading His words and living out the Gospel." Her daily morning prayer focuses on those Gospels that describe Jesus' interaction with the outcasts who had no one to speak for them and their needs. Her reflections have led her to see the interconnection between human rights, social equality and work for the poor all flowing from the dignity of the human person.

Reflection: The poor and vulnerable have a special place in Catholic social teaching.

Many people born in the United States grow up with their life centered on the consumption of material goods. As Bruce Malina reflects in contrasting a biblical perspective with contemporary times: "What one has, what one possesses, what one controls through ownership are far more important that what sort of person one is."[1] John F. Kavanaugh writes in *(Still) Following Christ in a Consumer Society*: "When consumerism becomes a full-blown philosophy and way of life, all social depersonalization, whether in violence or degradation, carries a common theme. Women and men are reduced to the status of means and instruments, whether it be for profit, for 'enlightened' self or national interest, or for pleasure."[2]

The vulnerable occupied a special place in Jesus' ministry. He himself was born in poverty, but as Scripture scholar John Meier points out, being a Palestinian peasant allows for a wide range of meanings.[3] It can be ascertained at least, that Jesus had to work hard at his living as a woodworker before he began his public ministry. As related in Luke's gospel Jesus was born in a stable since there was no room for Mary and Joseph in the place where travelers lodged (see Luke 2:7) His lifestyle evidenced that he was a man with few earthly possessions.

Once, as Jesus neared Jerusalem, three people who wanted initially to be his followers approached him. They wanted to follow Jesus, but had a certain hesitation. Each had important responsibilities that made perfect sense: (1) the necessity of home and place, (2) sacred duties, including the burial of one's parents, (3) relationships with family.[4] Jesus indicates some priorities for discipleship: "Foxes have lairs, the birds of the sky have nests, but the Son of Man has nowhere to lay his head" (Lk 9:58). He tells all who would be his follower that the call of his kingdom is indeed an absolute one. To follow him demands living "outside the system of producing and consuming. . . ."[5] Such a commitment can even put family obligations into perspective: "Family, marriage, and children are commonly used as avoidances and excuses for not walking a spiritual path. Jesus says, 'Don't turn back. Don't waver. You must keep moving ahead.'"[6] Such a way of life was to be part of the apostolic requirements. In fact, he was to tell Pontius Pilate, when questioned about his kingdom, that it was not of this world (see Jn 18:36). His kingdom is not based on force but rather on the hearts of men and women. Seek first the Kingdom of God. Belonging to this Kingdom will not be based on material advantage. As related in the beatitudes, how blessed are the poor in spirit, for the Kingdom of heaven will be theirs (Mt 5:3). Don't lay up for yourselves an earthly treasure. "Moths and rust corrode; thieves break in and steal" (Mt 6:19). Rather, Jesus warns, store up heavenly treasure. See God's care and love and know how valued you are. This is the treasure that lasts. "You cannot give yourself to God and money" (Mt 6:24).

The U.S. Catholic bishops have reminded us often that the poor and vulnerable people have a special place in Catholic social teaching acknowledging the privileged place of the poor in its life and mission.[7] Two gospels vie for the soul of the Christian in the Western World. "One form of life, one gospel, reveals men and women as replaceable and marketable commodities; another gospel, inalterably opposed to the first, reveals persons as irreplaceable and uniquely free beings."[8] Even with formal membership in a Christian church, it is often a temptation to follow the gospel of the culture.

Reflection: The gospel calls
Christians to put the needs of
the poor first.

Jesus welcomed all, including and perhaps, most especially, the poor, who perhaps best appreciated his invitation.

"Come to me all you who are weary and find life burdensome. Take my yoke upon your shoulders and learn from me, for I am gentle and humble of heart. Your souls will find rest, for my yoke is easy and my burden light"(Mt 11:29–30). As the U.S. bishops remind us, economic life is an important area where we live out our faith. "The life and words of Jesus and the teachings of his Church call us to serve those in need and to work actively for social and economic justice."[9]

"Our dependence upon our material wealth has become part of our identity. It has become almost impossible to imagine any other approach to life, because it has become life itself for us. The Commodity Form has become gospel. But that does not mean it has become good news."[10]

Reflection: A basic moral test for society is how its most vulnerable members are faring.

Recent popes including Pope John Paul II have addressed the widening gap between rich and poor, the so-called developed North and developing South. John Paul has lamented the inability of developing nations to become more self-supporting due to international debt. Added to this is the refugee problem—millions who are deprived of home, employment, family and homeland. The U.S. bishops attempted to provide some criteria for helping Americans appreciate their responsibility to the poor within our own borders. Using biblical and theological themes, the bishops provide an important perspective on economic ethics:

- **Love and solidarity**: The commandments to love God with all our hearts and to love our neighbor as oneself point out the way to true human fulfillment. "Only active love of God and neighbor makes the fullness of community happen. Christians look forward in hope to a true communion among all persons with each other and with God.[11]

- **Justice and participation:** Christians strive to fulfill biblical justice. Such an understanding includes the fullness of love, compassion, holiness, and peace. The bishops reiterate the teaching of the Second Vatican Council (*Pastoral Constitution on the Church, Gaudium et Spes*, no. 69): "The right to have a share of earthly goods sufficient for oneself and one's family belongs to everyone. The fathers and doctors of the church held this view, teaching that we are obliged to come to the relief of the poor and to do so not merely out of our superfluous goods."

- **Overcoming marginalization and powerlessness:** All people, by virtue of basic justice, are entitled to minimum levels of participation in the life of the community. "The ultimate injustice is for a person or group to be treated actively or abandoned passively as if they were nonmembers of the human race."[12] It can happen that even within the United States, individuals, families and local communities become victims to economic forces that are beyond their control, that results in a downward cycle of poverty. "The poor, the disabled, and the unemployed too often are simply left behind."[13] This also happens, as we know, beyond our borders, in least developed countries where conditions are often more severe.

"Whole nations are prevented from fully participating in the international economic order because they lack the power to change their disadvantaged position."[14] The actions by which a few, elite of a particular country exclude the majority from participation in the meager resources available in the homeland, has sometimes been referred to as a form of "social sin." The unwillingness of Christians at times to remedy such situations when knowledgeable of them, can likewise be called a sinful dereliction of one's Christian duty. "Stated positively, justice demands that social institutions be ordered in a way that guarantees all persons the ability to participate actively in the economic, political, and cultural life of society."[15]

Christians are encouraged to set limits on how material goods are viewed, and Americans especially are summoned to develop an "inner freedom" to resist the temptation to seek more. Pope John Paul II has asked how any government could justify huge sums of money being used for the increased stockpiling of weapons that should be used for increasing the development of peoples? He has further identified two signs of underdevelopment that need to be addressed by developed nations: *housing* and *unemployment*. According to John Paul, millions of people lack adequate housing due to urbanization, and in many countries, the opportunities for employment are shrinking.

The U.S. bishops have succinctly delineated a Christian economic perspective: "Every economic decision and institution must be judged in light of whether it protects or undermines the dignity of the human person."[16]

---

*Reflection: The lesson of the
parable of the Last Judgment is
that we will be judged on our
treatment of others.*

Jesus proposed an evaluation for assessing one's discipleship in the parable of the Last Judgment (Mt. 25:31–46). Here is pictured the king addressing those blessed because they have done acts of mercy for "one of these least brothers of mine" and therefore have done them for him. This sequence is followed by the king admonishing those who are accursed, since they failed to see the king in their brothers and sisters in need. The lesson of the parable seems unambiguous: Jesus will judge us according to the way in which we have reacted to human need. "As Christians, we are called to respond to the needs of our sisters and brothers, but those with the greatest needs require the greatest response."[17] It is clear in examining the ministry of Jesus, that he had a concentrated mission to all those who would be considered by society as "the outsider."

This parable poses a daunting hurdle: "We are amazed at his treatment of the mentally ill, including men, women, and even children in distress, as well as those believed to be possessed by demons. We are perhaps more astonished at his relationship with the morally deviant: criminals and quislings, adulterers and prostitutes, but also the contaminated and the ritually impure. From tax collectors to menstruating women. All these— and all women in particular—were among the poor."[18] Jesus came to reverse what were the acceptable priorities: "[T]hose who were currently 'the first' would, in fact be last, masters would become servants, the self-righteous would be condemned, the exalted would be humbled, glut would turn to hunger, laughter to tears, and riches to impoverishment. To many who heard this message, this was good news indeed. But the very same words were anything but good news to the insider participants to whom Jesus also delivered the message."[19] It is our treatment of just such people and how we have accepted them, that will serve as the criterion for entrance into the kingdom of God. "I was a stranger and you welcomed me" (Mt 25:35). I took in, gave drink, gave food, visited those who were marginalized by society. But the Christian must be willing to become the receiver as well, who welcomes the ministry of others, who gives up control and power and identifies with the outcast: "In our zeal to respond to Jesus the stranger by casting ourselves in the role of savior, we may have missed the implications: that we are called to be *as he was*, and that being a stranger was an intentional part of who he was. He did not cling to his equality with God but emptied himself. He was born as an outsider, chose to live as one and accepted the ultimate humiliation of crucifixion outside the gate or city wall: the quintessential mark of the outsider."[20]

The Christian religion is not only a religion of knowledge and of contemplation. It is a religion of "God's action and man's action. That great master of mystical life and contemplation, Saint John of the Cross has written: 'At the evening of our life we will be judged on love' (*The Sayings of Light and Love*, 57)."[21]

Reflection: Our tradition calls us to put the needs of the poor and the vulnerable first.

The church's concern for the poor flows from "the Gospel of the Beatitudes, of the poverty of Jesus and of his concern for the poor. Love for the poor is even one of the motives for the duty of working so as to 'be able to give to those in need.' It extends not only to material poverty but also to the many forms of cultural and religious poverty."[22] As the U.S. bishops stated in *Everyday Christianity: To Hunger and Thirst for Justice, A Pastoral Reflection on Lay Discipleship for Justice in a New Millennium:* "Every believer is called to serve the 'least of these,' to 'hunger and thirst for justice,' to be a 'peacemaker.' Catholics are called by God to protect human life, to promote human dignity, to defend the poor and to seek the common good. This social mission of the church belongs to all of us. It is an essential part of what it is to be a believer."[23]

Social justice is built up or torn down each day by the countless decisions and choices we make. ". . . [The] vocation to pursue justice is not simply an individual task—it is a call to work with others to humanize and shape the institutions that touch so many people."[24]

Reflection: As Christians, we are called to respond to the needs of all our sisters and brothers, but those with the greatest needs require the greatest response.

The Letter of James is a sharp rebuke to those who would fail in their responsibility to share their riches. In chapter five, James illustrates the worthlessness of material possessions in the ultimate scheme of life. His other aim is to show the unseemly character of those who horde their riches. He excoriates the three main sources of wealth in his day: corn and grain, garments, gold and silver. All three will ultimately rot. James "pulls no punches" in calling the rich to accountability:

> Come now, you rich people, weep and wail for the miseries that are coming to you. Your riches have rotted, and your clothes are moth-eaten. Your gold and silver have rusted, and their rust will be evidence against you, and it will eat your flesh like fire. You have laid up treasure for the last days. Listen! The wages of the laborers who mowed your fields, which you kept back by fraud, cry out, and the cries of the harvesters have reached the ears of the Lord of hosts. You have lived on the earth in luxury and in pleasure; you have fattened your hearts in a day of slaughter. You have condemned and murdered the righteous one, who does not resist you (Jas 5:1–6).

It is James's conviction that when material possessions are the motivating and sole rationale for one's life, it is illusionary, since these possessions are all destined for decay. It requires the development of a strong Christian conscience with moral values to effect a helpful change. It was the bishops' hope when they wrote their pastoral letter on the economy that it would stimulate a national debate on the economy. It was their further hope that the poor would benefit from such a discussion. "The life and dignity of millions of men, women and children hang in the balance. Decisions must be judged in light of what they do *for* the poor, what they do *to* the poor, and what they enable the poor to do *for themselves*. The fundamental moral criterion for all economic decisions, policies, and institutions is this: They must be at the service of *all people, especially the poor.*"[25] The bishops present their readers a stark challenge: "No one may claim the name Christian and be comfortable in the face of the hunger, homelessness, insecurity, and injustice found in the country and the world."[26] The bishops seek a broad consensus and the participation of many constituencies in their work to combat this injustice: "We seek the cooperation and support of those who do not share our faith or tradition. The common bond of humanity that links all persons is the source of our belief that the country can attain a renewed moral vision. The questions are basic and the answers are often elusive; they challenge us to serious and sustained attention to economic justice."[27]

Reflection: Whenever there is structural injustice, Christians are called to oppose it.

Our baptismal call is a commitment to service in the works of mercy, actions by which we assist our neighbor in obtaining spiritual and corporal necessities. Such activity includes instructing, advising, consoling and comforting (spiritual works); feeding the hungry, sheltering the homeless, clothing the naked, visiting the sick and imprisoned, and burying the dead (corporal works of mercy). Again, the letter of James is instructive, with many practical suggestions. His letter is replete with references to the connection of the profession of faith and practice, matching words with deeds. In chapter two he presents a man with no clothes to protect him from the elements, and no food to eat. It is not sufficient to wish him well and express deepest sympathies for his plight.

> If a brother or sister has nothing to wear
> and no food for the day, and you say to
> them, "Goodbye and good luck! Keep
> warm and well fed," but do not meet their
> bodily needs, what good is that? (Jas
> 2:15–16).

Sympathy without some effort at practical means to alleviate the suffering of a brother or sister in need is useless. James would teach that faith without works is dead. As Barclay comments on this famous passage: "In his approach to this subject, James is profoundly right. There is nothing more dangerous than the repeated experiencing of a fine emotion with no attempt to put it into action. It is a fact that every time a man feels a noble impulse without taking action, he becomes less likely ever to take action. An emotion is not something in which to luxuriate; it is something which at the cost of effort and of toil and of discipline and of sacrifice must be turned into the stuff of life."[28]

To help those in need, it is often required to work towards structural change in society. This is not the prerogative only of government officials. In fact, the church has reminded governments that each substratum of society has an appropriate role. "The need for vital contributions from different human associations—ranging in size from the family to government—has been classically expressed in Catholic social teaching in the principle of subsidiarity."[29] Subsidiarity has been defined by Pope Pius XI in his classical encyclical, *Quadragesimo Anno*:

> Just as it is gravely wrong to take from
> individuals what they can accomplish by
> their own initiative and industry and give
> it to the community, so also it is an injus-

tice and at the same time, a grave evil and disturbance of right order to assign to a greater and higher association what lesser and subordinate organizations can do. For every social activity ought of its very nature to furnish help (*subsidium*) to the members of the body social, and never destroy and absorb them.[30]

The principle of subsidiarity is constructive for economic dialogue in society. "It [subsidiarity] provides space for freedom, initiative, and creativity on the part of many social agents. At the same time, it insists that *all* these agents should work in ways that help build up the social body. Therefore, in all their activities these groups should be working in ways that express their distinctive capacities for action, that help meet human needs, and that make true contributions to the common good of the human community."[31]

The pursuit of justice for the poor must be the work of everyone in society: "The task of creating a more just U.S. economy is the vocation of all and depends on strengthening the virtues of public service and responsible citizenship in personal life and on all levels of institutional life."[32] For example, public authorities are called to further the social progress for the benefit of all citizens. While observing subsidiarity (governments should undertake only those initiatives that exceed the capacity of individuals or private groups acting independently: one should not do what can be done by the smaller unit of society well), public authorities can make sure that employment is provided for as many workers as possible, since full employment is the foundation of a just economy. There are many people today who do not have the means that would enable them to take their place within a productive system in which work is truly central. "They have no way of entering the network of knowledge and intercommunication which would enable them to see their qualities appreciated and utilized. Thus, if not actually exploited, they are to a great extent marginalized; economic development takes place over their heads, so to speak, when it does not actually reduce the already narrow scope of their old subsistence economies."[33] Likewise, public authorities must make sure that a just balance between wages and prices is maintained and the goods and services for a better life are provided to as many people as possible:

> Many other people, while not completely marginalized, live in situations in which the struggle for a bare minimum is uppermost. These are situations in which the rules of the earliest periods of capitalism still flourish in conditions of "ruthlessness" in no way inferior to the darkest moments of the first phase of industrialization. In other cases, the land is still the central element in the economic process, but those who cultivate it are excluded from ownership and are reduced to a state of quasi-servitude. In these cases, it is still possible today, as in the days of *Rerum Novarum*, to speak of inhuman exploitation.[34]

Efforts should likewise be made to eliminate or to keep within bounds the inequalities that exist between different sectors of the economy, since the economy is at the service of the human being. No one is justified in keeping for his or her exclusive use what is not needed, when others lack basic necessities. Unfortunately, again as John Paul II points out, the great majority of people in the Third World still live in such conditions, with only the most meager of resources. Many solutions have been suggested, but few have worked. "Even in recent years it was thought that the poorest countries would develop by isolating themselves from the world market and by depending only on their own resources. Recent experience has shown that countries which did this have suffered stagnation and recession."[35]

The U.S. economy is marked by an uneven distribution of wealth and income. This distribution needs to be evaluated from a moral perspective. Are the basic needs of the poor being met? Are all levels of society participating in the economic life of the nation? Do all segments of society feel that they have some control over their lives? "Every citizen also has the responsibility to work to secure justice and human rights through an organized social response. According to Pius XI, 'Charity will never be true charity unless it takes justice into account. . . . Let no one attempt with small gifts of charity to exempt himself from the great duties imposed by justice.' The guaranteeing of basic justice for all is not an optional expression of largesse but an inescapable duty for the whole of society."[36]

All citizens, working together have a responsibility to assist in helping those outside the visible benefits of the economy: "More specifically, it is the responsibility of all citizens, acting through their government, to assist and empower the poor, the disadvantaged, the handicapped, and the unemployed."[37]

John Kavanaugh suggests several strategies that when undertaken by the committed Christian can help bring about a life and life style that can make structural changes:

- **Personal Life Choice and Centering on Jesus:** The Christian who wishes to follow Christ must be centered in Christ. Prayer is crucial, helping us know in depth the Master and Teacher who impacted the society in which he lived, by what he did always in relationship with his Father. Jesus often separated himself from his disciples for prayer, and it is clear that his actions flowed from his prayer. Prayer is the unfolding in our hearts of the knowledge that God is within. "Through prayer God reveals Himself above all as Mercy—that is, Love that goes out to those who are suffering, Love that sustains, uplifts, and invites us to trust. The victory of good in the world is united organically with this truth. A person who prays professes such a truth and in a certain sense makes God, who is merciful Love, present in the world."[38] Prayer can impart a new perspective on our culture's criterion for success: "Daily centering is an 'enabling' activity, whereby [one] becomes once again conscious of the irreplaceable present and [is extricated] from endless tapes about the past and endless rehearsals of the future."[39]

- **Style of Life:** Our prayerful relationship with God must flow forth in concrete lifestyles that reflect such intimacy. We begin to take on the mind of Christ. As Kavanaugh illustrates, interior dispositions and desires that flow from a serious relationship with Christ will be seen by such activities as not letting television be a surrogate life or a substitute for intimacy; living more simply, releasing oneself from the addiction of buying and consuming.[40]

- **Community:** One will experience the need to collaborate with others, to communicate one's faith, to take a stand against the imperatives of competition and individualism. Such a commitment will be seen in community activities of prayer, discussion, celebration, and social service.[41]

- **Social Justice:** There will be seen an increasing need to participate, even in some small way, in works of justice. It will be seen as important to become increasingly knowledgeable of particular issues that touch social justice and to take actions that can influence and impact the issues at hand.

- **The Gift of the Dispossessed:** It will also become increasingly important to know those who are marginalized in society, the dispossessed who were such a focus of Jesus' ministry. "The life of Jesus is not only that wherein we are saved, not only that by which we are instructed; it is also the very *way*, the very methodology, of Christian praxis."[42]

God of Justice,
open our eyes
to see you in the face of the poor.
Open our ears
to hear you in the cries of the exploited.
Open our mouths
to defend you in the public squares
as well as in private deeds.
Remind us that what we do
to the least ones,
we do to you.
Amen.[43]

Reflection Questions:

1. What possible solutions are proposed by the recent popes in dealing with the disparity in wealth, "North and South" and First, Second, and Third Worlds?

2. What are possible consequences of such disparity?

3. Where is such disparity seen in my own surroundings?

4. How does my lifestyle at the present time reflect my call to be "poor in spirit?"

5. What concrete action steps can I take in my own environment to actualize the call of the gospel to bring good news to the poor?

Chapter Six:
The Dignity of Work and the Rights of Workers

> "The ultimate meaning of life lies neither
> in work nor in play. A fulfilled life implies
> both meaningful leisure and honorable,
> socially relevant work. In the biblical
> sense, life is a feast manifesting its mean-
> ing and joy in all of life's dimensions."
> —*Bernard Häring*

Patrick D., while growing up in Syracuse, New York, learned at a young age of the struggles of earning a living when his father, a longtime employee of General Electric, was laid off as a cost-saving measure when his department was relocated to Mexico. With his father a member of the International Union of Electricians local 320 and other relatives members of the United Auto Workers he also learned quickly of the challenges of collective bargaining and union representation. His vocational decision to become involved in labor work and union organizing was set as early as high school. While he was attending a bioethics course, the teacher had remarked on the scientific advancements which one day could see genetic improvements in humans that could allow them to work in toxic environments. This concept so repulsed him that he found himself becoming increasingly oriented towards the protection of the individual and respect for the dignity of the person.

Since obtaining a degree in industrial relations from Le Moyne College he has worked as a labor relations specialist. He now works for New York State United Teachers in their regional office in Rochester, New York. He has been influenced by papal encyclicals such as **Rerum Novarum** *(1891) which addressed the issue of labor associations, as well as the pastoral letter of the U.S. Bishops,* **Economic Justice for All** *(1986) which he believed illustrated the proper balance between community need and industrial ownership. Such teachings, he believes, affirm his work and what he is doing: "church teachings have addressed the respectful and fair way in which workers and all people should be treated."*

He would describe his spirituality as "action and contemplation." He starts each day reflecting on the Scriptures proclaimed at Mass and he tries to open himself to the Holy Spirit's direction for the day. He has been assisted in his journey of faith by a regular meeting with a spiritual director and by frequently attending Bible studies. His prayer life has helped him to see his work as a natural extension into the world of his relationship with Jesus Christ, whom he appreciates for his tireless work to proclaim respect for the dignity of each person. He admits that he cannot now read the newspaper without being affected by the injustice he reads about, questioning himself about what he can do. He sees the Christian as being called "to set the tone for society, not to mirror society."

Jesus demonstrated the importance and dignity of labor in virtue of the fact that, like his father, he was a laborer, who worked with his hands. The worshippers in the synagogue were stunned when they heard Jesus, a common laborer, preach. "Where did this man get such wisdom . . . ? Isn't this the carpenter's son?" (Mt 13:54–55) John Meier prefers to describe Jesus as a "woodworker," because of the contemporary restricted usage of the term "carpenter." The term used in Matthew "could be applied to any worker who plied his trade 'with a hard material that retains its hardness throughout the operation, e.g., wood and stone or even horn or ivory.'"[1] Meier goes on to explain that some of Jesus' work would have involved carpentry in the narrow sense, e.g., woodwork in constructing parts of houses. ". . . Jesus would have made various pieces of furniture, such as beds, tables, stools, and lampstands (cf. 2 Kgs 4:10), as well as boxes, cabinets, and chests for storage."[2] Meier describes a vocation that required a broad variety of skills and talents, as well as labor that involved much sweat and muscle power.[3] Truly Jesus experienced a full range of activities of a laborer of his day and time.

The church since the pontificate of Pope Leo XIII has addressed the vocation of the worker and the dignity of labor. On May 15, 1891, Leo issued an encyclical on the plight of the worker and working conditions, *Rerum Novarum*, "of New Things." The encyclical spoke to a myriad of social problems of the age, including the possible creation of labor unions, the dignity of labor, and the need for better working conditions. It also stressed the need for greater collaboration between employer and employee to resolve the injustices that were especially experienced by the working class. The pope based his principles and teachings about employment and work-related issues on the dignity of the human person.

> What stands out and excels in us, what
> makes man man and distinguishes him
> generally from the brute, is the mind or
> reason. And owing to the fact that this ani-
> mal alone has reason, it is necessary that
> man have goods not only to be used,
> which is common to all living things, but
> also to be possessed by stable and perpetu-
> al right; and this applies not merely to
> those goods which are consumed by use,
> but to those also which endure after being
> used.[4]

The human person has been given the gift of reason by
the Creator, and can use the goods of the earth for the
achieving of certain ends. God gives the earth and its
benefits to the whole human race, and not to just a
select few. Naturally, human institutions are called upon
to make certain determinations about the limits of private possession, but this should not detract from the fact
that the earth should serve the common interests of all.
Those who are lacking certain resources supply labor
and thus are compensated for their work. The worker,
according to Leo, is to perform entirely and conscientiously whatever task has been agreed upon. But
employers have many obligations, as well as rights:

> Workers are not to be treated as slaves; jus-
> tice demands that the dignity of human
> personality be respected in them, ennobled
> as it has been through what we call the
> Christian character. If we hearken to natu-
> ral reason and to Christian philosophy,
> gainful occupations are not a mark of
> shame to man, but rather of respect, as

they provide him with an honorable
means of supporting life. It is shameful
and inhuman, however, to use men as
things for gain and to put no more value
on them than what they are worth in muscle and energy. Likewise, it is enjoined that
the religious interests and the spiritual
well-being of the workers receive proper
consideration.[5]

The pope also speaks of several duties of the employer:

Among the most important duties of
employers the principal one is to give
every worker what is justly due him.
Assuredly, to establish a rule of pay in
accord with justice, many factors must be
taken into consideration. But, in general,
the rich and employers should remember
that no laws, either human or divine, permit them for their own profit to oppress
the needy and the wretched or to seek gain
from another's want.[6]

Leo XIII declared the need for workers to have access to
associations which can provide an appropriate forum to
work with fellow laborers for material benefits which
flow from the work expended. Such associations should
make sure that adequate retirement benefits are provided. "In summary, let this be laid down as a general and
constant law: Workers' associations ought to be consti-
tuted and so governed as to furnish the most suitable
and most convenient means to attain the object proposed, which consists in this, that the individual members of the association secure, so far as possible, an
increase in the goods of body, of soul, and of
prosperity."[7]

Leo details the obligations and rights of the state in the proper regulation of the relationships between the owners and their employees. The state must protect the public welfare and provide for good order within the society. The state should help make sure that workers are saved from labor that is excessive and must also provide for tolerable working conditions. Proper days off and vacations should be assured. To prevent work stoppages, it is the responsibility of the state to anticipate and prevent those conditions that can result in strikes by workers.

> Labor which is too long and too hard and the belief that pay is inadequate not infrequently give workers cause to strike and become voluntarily idle. This evil, which is frequent and serious, ought to be remedied by public authority, because such interruptions of work inflicts damage not only upon employers and upon the workers themselves, but also injures trade and commerce and the general interest of the State; and since it is usually not far removed from violence and rioting, it very frequently jeopardizes public peace. In this matter it is more effective and salutary that the authority of the law anticipate and completely prevent the evil from breaking out by removing early the causes from which it would seem that conflict between employers and workers is bound to arise.[8]

When this encyclical was written, conditions in which many workers labored were difficult and relations between employers and employees were unsustainable. This encyclical was a strong effort by Leo to bring

Christian values into the field of labor, a witness of the gospel to the secular realm.

> Everyone according to his position ought to gird himself for the task, and indeed as speedily as possible, lest by delaying the remedy, the evil, which is already of vast dimensions, become incurable. Let those in charge of States make use of the provisions afforded by laws and institutions; let the rich and employers be mindful of their duties; let the workers, whose cause is at stake, press their claims with reason. And since religion alone, as We said at the beginning, can remove the evil, root and branch, let all reflect upon this: First and foremost Christian morals must be reestab-lished, without which even the weapons of prudence, which are considered especially effective, will be of no avail to secure well-being."[9]

Pope John Paul II, writing on the ninetieth anniversary of the publication of *Rerum Novarum,* reiterated some of these same concerns in *Laborem Exercens, (On Human Work).* He acknowledged the contribution the Christian faith can make to the world of work and to the issues of labor in the modern workforce. To labor is actually to participate in the work of the Creator. "The word of God's revelation is profoundly marked by the funda-mental truth that *man,* created in the image of God, *shares by his work in the activity of the Creator* and that, within the limits of his own human capabilities, man in a sense continues to develop that activity and perfects it as he advances further and further in the discovery of the resources and values contained in the whole of creation."[10] In addition, the truth that Christian faith brings in Jesus Christ ennobles labor since he himself belonged to the working world. "It can indeed be said the *he looks with love upon human work* and the different forms that it takes, seeing in each one of these forms a particular facet of man's likeness with God, the Creator and Father."[11]

As the bishops of the United States have recently proclaimed: "Work is more than a way to make a living; it is a form of continuing participation in God's creation. If the dignity of work is to be protected, then the basic rights of workers must be respected—the right to productive work, to decent and fair wages, to organize and join unions, to private property, and to economic initiative."[12]

Reflection: Work is an expression of our dignity and our involvement in God's creation.

Pope John Paul II has had firsthand experience of the world of hard labor. He performed much manual labor, including work in a stone quarry in 1940, then the following year in a water purification facility in the same plant, during the Nazi occupation of Poland during World War II. As George Weigel recounts, this was difficult work: "Although Karol Wojtyla would later mine his experience of the quarry for his literary, philosophical, and theological purposes, the fact remains that this was hard and dangerous work. Every day, each worker had to fill one of the small tramcars with limestone. . . . The limestone still had to be broken up and shoveled, hour after hour."[13] As the pope recounts in his memoir, *Gift and Mystery*, this experience greatly affected him. "Having worked with my hands, I knew quite well the meaning of physical labor. Every day I had been with people who did heavy work. I came to know their living situations, their families, their interests, their human worth and their dignity."[14] While engaged in doctoral studies in Rome after his ordination to the priesthood, he visited France and Belgium where he became interested in the worker-priest movement that was underway in these countries. "Only later as a priest, during my studies in Rome, when my colleagues at the Belgian College made me aware of the issue of worker-priests and the Young Christian Worker movement (JOC), did I realize how important contact with the world of work had become for the Church and the priesthood in the West. This contact was already a part of my life experience."[15]

The thought of John Paul II about labor was more recently influenced by the *Pastoral Constitution on the Church*, (*Gaudium et Spes*). Work is the fulfillment of man's vocation to exercise dominion over the earth in the design and plan of the Creator:

> Throughout the course of the centuries, men have labored to better the circumstances of their lives through a monumental amount of individual and collective effort. To believers, this point is settled: considered in itself, such human activity accords with God's will. For man, created to God's image, received a mandate to subject to himself the earth and all that it contains, and to govern the world with justice and holiness; a mandate to relate himself and the totality of things to Him who was to be acknowledged as the Lord and Creator of all. Thus, through the

> dominion of all things by man, the name
> of God would be made wonderful through
> all the earth.
> This holds good also for even the most
> ordinary everyday activities. For, while
> providing the substance of life for them-
> selves and their families, men and women
> are performing their activities in a way
> which appropriately benefits society. They
> can justly consider that by their labor they
> are unfolding the Creator's work, serving
> their brothers and sisters, and contributing
> by their personal industry to the realiza-
> tion in history of the divine plan.[16]

Thus labor can be seen as God's design for human
beings. Through work, they realize their potential and
give glory to God. ". . . [C]hristians are convinced that
the triumphs of the human race are a sign of God's
greatness and the flowering of His own mysterious
design. For the greater man's power becomes, the farther his individual and community responsibility
extends."[17] The Christian message encourages rather
than discourages humanity to undertake labor in order
to build up the world.

---

*Reflection: Work is more than a
way to make a living; it is an
expression of our dignity and a
form of continuing participation
in God's creation.*

In Catholic teaching, work can be seen both as a right
and as a duty. "It is a right because work is how we
express our dignity and provide for ourselves and our
families. Work is necessary to help use the earth's

resources to benefit each of us and all of society. Through work we contribute to God's continuing creation. Indeed, work helps to direct human activity toward God. In the words of Saint Paul, 'Whatever you do, do all to the glory of God' (1 Cor 10:31)."[18]

During this last century, the Catholic church has broadened its notion of labor, to see more fully its impact on issues of economic life. "Our Catholic tradition holds that 'human work is a key, probably the essential key, to the whole social question' (*Laborem Exercens no. 3)* facing society."[19] We are called to confront a development within the economy that results when a substantial number of people who are left behind, unable to escape poverty. "The values of our faith call us to shape economic policies that protect human dignity, promote strong families, and create vibrant communities. In our religious tradition the fundamental moral test of any society is how the poor, the weak, and the vulnerable are faring."[20]

> The church proposes that our social relationships are not determined purely on the basis of economic factors. When we work, we utilize the talents and gifts that the Creator has given to us. Furthermore, work is also redemptive. The laborer shows him or herself to be a "disciple of the Christ by carrying the cross daily, in the work . . . [the person] is called to accomplish. Work can be a means of sanctification and a way of animating earthly realities with the Spirit of Christ" (C.C.C., no. 2427).

Catholic teaching on work is based on the principle that people are more important than things. "In Catholic social teaching, work is for the person, not the person for work. "[21] Despite the remarkable changes in technology the theme of work continues to be a major focus of our national agenda.

Today there are many low-wage workers who are both seeking to obtain meaningful employment as well as trying to achieve self-sufficiency. They are finding it increasingly difficult to meet their own needs and the needs of their families. The welfare system in the United States, in attempting to restructure its orientation, has focused on finding work and has reduced the welfare rolls significantly. "But enthusiasm for falling welfare numbers should be tempered by the reality of persistent poverty and wages too meager to provide for a family's needs. Many may be leaving welfare; too few have left poverty."[22] Since some low-wage earners in industry are from abroad without permanent legal status, a legalization program would help protect their basic labor rights and "ensure that workers in the United States are afforded a living wage and decent working conditions."[23]

Since economic life involves a variety of various interests, it is not surprising that there are conflicts typical to employment. "Efforts should be made to reduce these conflicts by negotiation that respects the rights and duties of each social partner: those responsible for business enterprises, representatives of wage earners (for example, trade unions), and public authorities when appropriate" (C.C.C., no. 2430). It is consistent with the teachings of the gospel that the rights and interests of workers be protected as much and as fully as possible. ". . . [W]orkers, particularly those in the growing service industry, must be assured of their right to choose whether to organize and join unions or other associations to promote and defend their dignity. The church has long stood and continues to stand with workers and their unions in the struggle for justice, decent wages and a meaningful voice in economic life."[24]

Workers, many a part of organized labor, have given much to the United States over the last century. "Yet American unions never capitulated to the concept of 'class struggle' that found such fertile ground in the rest of the industrial world. Union leaders instead saw their organization as part of the American experiment in democracy, and urged their membership to seek social justice for all instead of class struggle."[25] Such concerns invite all Christians to search for social justice by working towards public policies that protect and promote strong families and create decent jobs.

The worker has the duty to perform conscientiously whatever duties voluntarily and equitably are agreed to. It is also expected that the employee will not injure the property nor do harm to the employer. The employer must see the worker as a person, and not as a "thing" or "object" that assists the employer in making a profit. Employers must give to those who work for them what they are justly due.

Reflection: People have the right to decent and productive work, to decent and fair wages, to private property and economic initiative.

Cardinal Roger Mahony, as chairman of the Domestic Policy Committee of the United States Conference of Catholic Bishops, in a Labor Day statement in 2000, further identified what the U.S. bishops had previously described as three economies living side by side (U.S.C.C.B., *A Decade After Economic Justice for All*, 1996):

- A **first economy**, that finds many people prospering in the information age and global marketplace.

- A **second economy**, including people who are doing well by some measures, but are affected by declining incomes, struggles to afford appropriate health care, and worries about the cost of a college education or Catholic schools for their children.

- A **third economy** which affects a substantial number of people, left behind and unable to escape poverty. They live in neighborhoods where there are no decent jobs nor is there affordable housing.[26]

Although the *first economy* has been impacted severely by the recent fluctuations in the stock market, the disparities in the three economies remain relatively intact.

It has been the teaching of the church that access to employment and to professions must be open to all, without unjust discrimination: men and women, healthy and disabled, natives and immigrants (cf. *Laborem Exercens, On the Ninetieth Anniversary of Rerum Novarum*, no. 19, 22–23). Furthermore, society is called upon to help it citizenry to find work and employment (cf. *Centesimus Annus, On the Hundredth Anniversary of Rerum Novarum*, no. 48).

A legitimate fruit of work done is the payment of a just wage. As stated in *The Church in the Modern World*: "Remuneration for work should guarantee man the opportunity to provide a dignified livelihood for himself and his family on the material, social, cultural and spiritual level, taking into account the role and the productivity of each, the state of the business, and the common good" (no. 67, §2). "As a nation we must ensure that everyone who works full [time] can earn enough to raise a family. The ongoing effort to raise the minimum wage . . . is a modest step toward that goal, but still insufficient . . . raising the minimum wage is just a beginning, but it is the least we should do."[27]

Governments are called to a special solicitude for workers and the protection of their rights. It may even be necessary for the state to intervene in labor relations (e.g., work stoppages) but only insofar as necessary, i.e., no farther than the remedy requires. The state may, in fact, be helpful in the avoidance of labor strikes and other worker protests by remedying those situations that lead to labor unrest by ensuring that laws properly restrict the amount of hours worked, if they are more than humanly possible, establishing a minimum wage, and providing time for rest in the form of days off and vacations.

Reflection: Workers have the strong support of the church in forming and joining unions and worker associations of their choosing in the exercise of their dignity and rights.

It can be appropriate for workers to join in an association, to organize into a forum and be in a better position to assure an appropriate return in wages for work expended, as well as to assure adequate retirement benefits. Christian associations can be particularly helpful insofar as they provide opportunities for spiritual growth in the Christian life.

Workers also have the right to strike "when it cannot be avoided, or at least when it is necessary to obtain a proportionate benefit" (*C.C.C.*, no. 2435). However, it is not an absolute right. In fact, it becomes morally unacceptable "when accompanied by violence, or when objectives are included that are not directly linked to working conditions or are contrary to the common good" (*C.C.C.*, no. 2435). In some respects guided by the social teachings of the church to vindicate basic human rights, the workers of Poland were able to launch a labor union against the wishes of the Communist government in 1980 (Solidarity). "It should not be a surprise that Pope John Paul II, a former archbishop of Krakow and a major supporter of Solidarity, has been an indefatigable defender and promoter of the interests of workers."[28]

Reflection: These values are at the heart of Rerum Novarum, and other encyclicals on economic justice.

Pope Leo XIII laid the foundations for church teachings in the area of labor and labor management in his encyclical *Rerum Novarum*, issued in 1891. Leo begins his teaching by placing the question of labor within the context of the person and his or her natural dignity. What makes the human person unique is the ability to reason. Each person uses his or her reason to achieve desired ends, or goals. Each individual is called to use his or her goods for the best possible good. The earth's resources are not for the exclusive use of any individual or country, but for the common interest of all.

It was the hope of Leo XIII that the rich and poor, workers and employers, citizens and the state would not be seen as adversaries. It was also Leo's hope that by reminding and calling each segment of society to a recognition of their rights and obligations, the church could bring together the various actors in the world of labor.

He also wanted to remind the industrial leaders in the advancing technological and industrial age that workers were not to be treated as slaves and were always to be treated with human dignity. He deplored the use of people as things for gain. He reminded employers of the need to ensure that workers could take proper care of their families with a just wage paid.

> *Reflection: In Catholic teaching, the economy exists to serve people, not the other way around.*

One of the first encyclicals issued by Pope John Paul II was on labor, *Laborem Exercens*. Even though popes had previously addressed this topic (notably, as mentioned, Leo XIII), he found it important to bring this topic to the attention of society again, especially within the context of advances in technology, the economy and politics. As we have seen, work, according to John Paul, is a fundamental part of the life of the person. Each individual is made in the image and likeness of God and is capable of working in a way that realizes the self, leading to fulfillment as a human being. Repeating Leo XIII's teaching about the role of labor, John Paul would also remind us that the person is destined for work and not the work for the person. The person must never be seen as just an instrument of production. Paramount is the honoring and respect for the dignity of the laborer.

John Paul in his pontificate has always been sensitive to human rights and this sensitivity is seen in his promotion of the rights of workers. Such an approach stresses that the machinery of labor and the resultant economy serves humanity and not the other way around. The right of association, by which workers band together for common useful objectives, is to be respected, to make sure that no workers are exploited. But the means that are used at times to achieve common objectives, such as work stoppages, are not to be abused. Benefits such as medical assistance, health and retirement should be provided as well as days off and vacations. A safe working environment must also be provided. The government must also do all within its power to make sure that a responsible labor policy is practiced, that suitable employment is found for all those who are capable of working. No one must be discriminated against for the jobs the person would be capable of performing. Each socioeconomic system is judged on how well the worker's labor is remunerated.

> Creator God,
> thank you for providing us
> with the gift to share our talents.
> Provide our community, our nation, our
>   world
> the fortitude to provide work for all
> which is decent and fair.
> Make us faithful stewards
> of your creation
> to enhance the human dignity
> of our global family.
> We ask this in the name of Jesus,
> who lives and reigns
> with you and the Holy Spirit
> now and forever.
> Amen.[29]

Reflection Questions:

1. Why have recent popes considered issues of labor to be of such importance?

2. How do I look at my employment? How could I enhance my perspective of work?

3. Pope John Paul II speaks of a "spirituality of work." What are the spiritual dimensions of labor?

4. How can Christians counteract the "consumer" mentality that today concentrates so much on "having" rather than "being?"

5. Are there other criteria besides "profitability" that should be used in analyzing business success?

Chapter Seven:
Solidarity

"How beautiful will be the day when a
new society
instead of selfishly hoarding and keeping,
apportions, shares and divides up and all
rejoice
because we all feel we are children of the
same God!"

—*Oscar Romero*

*Eugene F. was born in College Point, New York, August 11,
1919. After attending St. Fidelis grammar school and then
Newtown high school, he enrolled for studies at Cornell
University where he received his B.S. in Physical Sciences
(and also met his future wife, Marie). After obtaining his
degree he taught science for one year before he left for industry. He obtained a job at Haloid Corporation (later Xerox)
where he was employed in a variety of capacities, including
research and product development. After experiencing some
health problems, he decided to retire at the age of fifty-seven.*

He had been active in several capacities at his parish, St. Margaret Mary in Rochester, New York, including eucharistic minister and chair of the parish council, when he decided to begin studies for the permanent diaconate. Ordained in 1983, his entire diaconal ministry was exercised at a local hospital, assisting where needed with his wife, Marie.

In a gradual, but strongly developed awareness, he came to suspect the motives for the first Iraqi war in 1990. The next several years saw his increasing involvement in reading, protesting and writing editorials against violence, which he has continued, including the recent Iraqi War (2003). "Violence promotes poverty, hate, greed, and the moral disease of nations' competition, which is used to dominate and resolve conflicts" says Gene. To combat the spirit of violence he has joined such organizations as Pax Christi, Fellowship of Reconciliation, and Faith and Resistance.

The basis for Gene's opposition to the violence of war comes from the message of the Scriptures which he prays over every day. "You cannot read the gospels without appreciating the message of compassion, so evident in Jesus' teaching." His prayer and his work on behalf of peace have also seen a development in his image of God. Where once he thought of the Creator as a demanding, rigid father expecting compliance with a rigid moral system, he now sees God as a lover, filled with mercy and compassion. Through his spirituality he has also come to better integrate life issues such as abortion and the death penalty, the consistent life ethic approach.

In August 1980, several months after Pope John Paul II's first return trip as pope to his homeland, the government of Poland signed an agreement that would permit the legality of "Solidarity", Solidarnosć. Now, in the Gdansk shipyard where there had been much worker unrest, for the first time an independent, self-governing trade union was established, the first recognized in the communist world. It would be led by Lech Walesa, a one-time unemployed electrician. Although some biographers of Pope John II, including Tad Szulc, believe that it is difficult to establish with certainty linkage of the creation of the trade union with John Paul's first visit to Poland as pope, it is clear that it greatly assisted this development. "The sense of being protected by John Paul II, both as a perception and a reality, during the long decade of the Polish crisis was vital, psychologically and politically, in keeping the opposition movement alive and going."[1]

This theme of *solidarity* has been an emerging theme of Catholic social teaching. It is not only in the sphere of labor relations, where solidarity in spirit helps in the attainment of worker objectives such as just wage and appropriate benefits. It is also present in papal teachings about the responsibility of citizenry in each nation to work together for the common good. There should exist a basic solidarity among all citizens and from this sense of commonality flows a natural call to work together that all may benefit. "The exercise of solidarity within each society is valid when its members recognize one another as persons."[2] Concern should be exercised on behalf of those who have more towards those who have less: " Those who are more influential, because they have a greater share of goods and common services, should feel responsible for the weaker and be ready to share with them all they possess."[3] The disadvantaged within society must also contribute their part: "Those who are weaker . . . in the same spirit of solidarity, should not adopt a purely passive attitude or one that is destructive of the social fabric . . . [they] should do what they can for the good of all."[4]

Jesus taught that national boundaries cannot be a restriction imposed on the call to love our neighbor, for example, when he taught about the "Good Samaritan", the least expected by his hearers to show compassion to the wounded Jew (Lk 10:30–37). Jesus is to be seen in all people. Whatever we do to our neighbor, we do to him (see Mt 25:31–46). This respect must extend toward other nations and cultures as well.

Reflection: We are one human family, whatever our national, racial, ethnic, economic or ideological differences.

The church teaches a need for solidarity among all citizens and a responsibility for all to work together for the common good. As John Paul II surveys the world he sees some signs of development of this solidarity. For example, there seems to exist a growing sense of solidarity among the poor of the world, "their efforts to support one another, and their public demonstrations on the social scene which, without recourse to violence, present their own needs and rights in the face of the insufficiency or corruption of the public authority."[5] In this struggle, says John Paul, the church must align herself with the poor and "discern the justice of their requests and to help satisfy them, without losing sight of the good of groups in the context of the common good."[6]

This concern must also be acknowledged in international relationships as well. "Interdependence must be transformed into solidarity, based on the principle that the goals of creation are meant for all. That which human industry produces through the processing of raw materials, with the contribution of work, must serve equally for the good of all."[7]

Such a realignment of our vision—seeing other countries as collaborators rather than competitors, can reshape our national policies: ". . . the stronger and richer nations must have a sense of moral responsibility for the other nations, so that a real international system may be established which will rest on the foundation of the equality of all peoples and on the necessary respect for their legitimate differences."[8] The burden, the pope says, is not entirely on the wealthy nations: "The economically weaker countries, or those still at subsistence level, must be enabled, with the assistance of other peoples and of the international community, to make a contribution of their own to the common good with their treasures of humanity and culture, which otherwise would be lost forever."[9]

The harmony in personal relations that should exist between people, proclaimed by the gospel, comes from a respect for each human person, regardless of nationality or country of origin. When we as a nation are tempted to look inward to our needs and priorities, it sometimes results in a feeling of indifference or a spirit of isolationism. Solidarity, believes John Paul, leads us to a greater understanding and appreciation of our unity in Christ. "Solidarity helps us to see the 'other'— whether a person, people or nation—not just as some kind of instrument, with a work capacity and physical strength to be exploited at low cost and then discarded when no longer useful, but as our 'neighbor,' a helper (cf. Gn 2:18–20), to be made a sharer, on a par with ourselves, in the banquet of life to which all are equally invited by God."[10]

---

*Reflection: We are our brothers'
and sisters' keepers (Gn 4:9).*

We are truly our brothers' and sisters' keepers.
"Learning to practice the virtue of solidarity means
learning that 'loving our neighbor' has global dimensions in our interdependent world."[11] The virtue of such
solidarity was explained by John Paul II: "a firm and
persevering determination to commit oneself to the
common good; that is to say, to the good of all and of
each individual, because we are all really responsible for
all" (*For the Twentieth Anniversary of Populorum
Progressio, Sollicitudo Rei Socialis*, no. 38). We become
practitioners of solidarity when we recognize the dignity of each person, that also reminds us of our commonality.

---

*Reflection: In a linked and limit-
ed world, our responsibilities to
one another cross national and
other boundaries.*

The phenomenon of technical and scientific achievement of the last few years makes communication to dis-
tant locations an immediate reality with satellites, faxes,
Internet and other technologies. This development has
been helpful in business and commercial transactions
that, for almost every major company, involve transna-
tional initiatives. We see live television reports from
around the world when there is "breaking news."
However, the analyses that often accompany these
reports rarely promote an understanding of the culture
involved in the story. Any cultural differences are
ignored, or used to explain how such differences can

lead to misunderstanding, and even violence. Rarely do these reports and analyses show our commonality, our interdependence and our need to understand and appreciate cultural differences.

One of the deplorable developments in recent years is the use of religion or religious beliefs to justify violence and acts of terrorism. The United States itself became victim to such an approach on September 11, 2001, when the World Trade Center was attacked by commandeered passenger aircraft. As the U.S. bishops pointed out in their pastoral message of November 14, 2001, terrorism is not a new problem, "but this terrorist threat is unique because of its global dimensions and the sheer magnitude of the terror its authors are willing and able to unleash. It is also new for us because we have not experienced war-like acts of violence on our own soil for many decades."[12] Sadly, it illustrates the continuing loss of a respect for human life. "Those who committed these atrocities do not distinguish between ordinary civilians and military combatants, and there is the threat of possible terrorist use of chemical, biological and nuclear weapons."[13]

Terrorist attacks against the United States in the last few years by some elements of Islamic fundamentalism have forced some Americans to try and understand Islam. It would seem that the terrorists, in this case, have been identified with an extreme understanding of the Islamic faith. The perception of the ideology of a few has caused great damage to our Christian understanding of Islam. "We are particularly troubled that some who engage in and support this new form of terror seek to justify it in part, as a religious act. Regrettably, the terrorists' notion of a religious war is inadvertently reinforced by those who would attribute the extremism of a few to Islam as a whole or who suggest that religion, by its nature, is a

source of conflict."[14] An appropriate response to terrorism of the kind witnessed September 11 comes from our
own religious tradition, "from the witness of so many
people of faith who have been a powerful force for non-
violent human liberation around the world."[15] In addition, a better appreciation and understanding of the role
that religion plays in world affairs is needed. "More
should be done at all levels to deepen and to broaden . . .
dialogue [between Christian and Muslim faiths] and
common action."[16] It is only in this way, says John Paul
II, that we can effectively work to counter the threat of
terrorism. "The various Christian confessions, as well as
the world's great religions need to work together to
eliminate the social and cultural causes of terrorism.
They can do this by teaching the greatness and dignity
of the human person and by spreading a clearer sense of
the oneness of the human family."[17]

Hopefully as we study Islam, we will see better the features of this religion that has common roots with our
own theological tradition. "The Church also has a high
regard for the Muslims, who worship one God, living
and subsistent, merciful and omnipotent, the Creator of
heaven and earth." (Vatican Council II, *Nostra Aetate,* no.
3). It is impossible not to admire the Islamic fidelity to
prayer: "The image of believers in Allah who, without
caring about time or place, fall to their knees and
immerse themselves in prayer remains a model for all
those who invoke the true God, in particular for those
Christians who, having deserted their magnificent
cathedrals, pray only a little or not at all."[18] John Paul II
was well aware of the challenges also present in
Christian-Islamic relations. Nevertheless, he would say,
". . . the Church remains always open to dialogue and
cooperation."[19]

A common thread of both the pope and bishops in offering a response to terrorism is an invitation to heartfelt prayer.

> . . . [P]rayer for peace is not an afterthought to the work of peace. It is of the very essence of building the peace of order, justice and freedom. To pray for peace is to open the human heart to the inroads of God's power to renew all things. With the life-giving force of his grace, God can create openings for peace where only obstacles and closures are apparent; he can strengthen and enlarge the solidarity of the human family in spite of our endless history of division and conflict. To pray for peace is to pray for justice, for a right ordering of relations within and among nations and peoples. It is to pray for freedom, especially for the religious freedom that is a basic human and civil right of every individual. To pray for peace is to seek God's forgiveness and to implore the courage to forgive those who have trespassed against us.[20]

Reflection: Violent conflict and the denial of dignity and rights to people anywhere in the globe diminish each of us.

When in 1961 John XXIII issued *Pacem in Terris*, his encyclical devoted to increasing understanding between nations, the world environment was steeped in the throes of the "cold war." The pope pleaded with nations to see what they had in common instead of just their differences. He began his encyclical by underscoring the importance of the person, and what natural law has taught about this dignity.

> By these laws men are most admirably taught, first of all how they should conduct their mutual dealings among themselves, then how the relationships between the citizens and the public authorities of each State should be regulated, then how States should deal with one another, and finally, how, on the one hand individual men and States, and on the other hand the community of all peoples, should act towards each other, the establishment of such a community being urgently demanded today by the requirements of universal common good.[21]

He was firmly convinced that respect for the individual could provide the basis for a movement towards understanding between people and nations. Each human being, endowed with intelligence and free will has written in the heart an order that is revealed in the conscience. He enumerates several rights that belong to each person: the right to life, to bodily integrity and the means suitable for the proper development of life: food, clothing, shelter, rest, medical care and necessary social services. Other rights he mentioned in this encyclical included: a good reputation, freedom in searching for truth and expressing and communicating opinions, the pursuit of art within the limits laid down by the moral order and common good.

The natural law also provides for other rights: to participate in the benefits of cultural life; the right to worship in accordance with one's conscience; and to practice religion both publicly and privately; to choose freely one's state in life, the right to establish a family and for parents to support and educate their children.

There exists as well the right to an opportunity to work and to good working conditions. The pope also taught that there was a right to participate in economic activities and to a wage determined by the criterion of justice and in keeping with the dignity of the human person. As has been taught by his predecessors, the pope also stated that there is also a right to private property.

There is as well the right of assembly and association, the freedom of movement and to emigrate when there is a just reason. There is a right to participate in political affairs and contribute to the common good. There should also be protection afforded to these rights according to the norm of law.

But John also taught concerning the inseparability of rights from *obligations*. Each member of society should strive to make sure that every citizen's rights are protected and observed. Christians have a particular obligation to infuse the culture by the light of faith and strength of love.

The bishops of the United States, in analyzing in depth the elements of world order that demanded attention in the quest for peace, reiterated the insights of Pope John XXIII in *Pacem in Terris*.

> The fundamental premise of world order
> in Catholic teaching is a theological truth:
> the unity of the human family—rooted in
> common creation, destined for the king-
> dom, and united by moral bonds of rights

and duties. This basic truth about the unity of the human family pervades the entire teaching on war and peace: for the pacifist position it is one of the reasons why life cannot be taken, while for the just-war position, even in a justified conflict bonds of responsibility remain in spite of the conflict.[22]

Reflection: This emerging theme of solidarity, so strongly articulated by Pope John Paul II, expresses the core of the church's concern for world peace, global development, environment, and international human rights.

With Christians working so that cultural, social, economic and political institutions are permeated with a spiritual value, as a "vivifying leaven in society," true peace can develop. As people grow in their appreciation of what they have in common, the better chance unity among people can develop. With the development of unity among peoples comes understanding and peace.

The bishops of the United States struggled in their pastoral letter, *The Challenge of Peace*, to confront the complex and difficult issue which is the greatest obstacle to solidarity among nations: war, specifically nuclear war. The center of the church's teaching on peace and the center of Catholic social teaching are the transcendence of God and the dignity of the human person. The Scriptures, both Hebrew and Christian, ground the task of peacemaking within a vision of God's kingdom. War and violence were a part of the history of the people of God, beginning with God's revelation to the people of

Israel. God would protect Israel from their enemies and lead them to victory in battle. But this image became gradually transformed with time. Peace would be experienced as God's gift; living in fidelity to the covenant given to them by their God, Israel would look to God as their security and their fortress.

In the Christian Scriptures, Jesus comes to proclaim the Kingdom of God, a kingdom that calls for a conversion of heart. After his resurrection, Jesus bestows a gift of peace, a gift that nobody can take away. The disciples are to become agents of reconciliation, making the peace that Jesus came to bring a reality, as they work to make this peace visible in their own communities. In being a community of justice, a true foundation will be provided for peace among people.

The church can provide solutions within its own area of competence: its teaching and its witness to that teaching. "The Church does not have technical solutions to offer for the problem of underdevelopment as such . . ." declared Pope John Paul II.[23] It is not within the competence of the church to suggest economic and political systems. Rather, the church, being an "expert in humanity," leads her to extend her mission to the various fields that occupy humankind in its search for happiness. "Following the example of my predecessors, I must repeat that whatever affects the dignity of individuals and peoples, such as authentic development, cannot be reduced to a technical problem. If reduced in this way, development would be emptied of its true content, and this would be an act of betrayal of the individuals and peoples whom development is meant to serve."[24]

The church's message in the area of development flows from the context of her mission to proclaim the Good News:

This is why the church has something to
say today, just as twenty years ago, and
also in the future, about the nature, conditions, requirements and aims of authentic
development and also about the obstacles
which stand in the way. In doing so the
church fulfills her mission to evangelize,
for she offers her first contribution to the
solution of the urgent problem of the
development when she proclaims the truth
about Christ, about herself and about man,
applying this truth to a concrete situation.[25]

For those who would attempt to characterize the
church's position on these matters as belonging to one
political camp or another, John Paul II assures that such
is not the case: "The Church's social doctrine is not a
'third way' between liberal capitalism and Marxist col-
lectivism, nor even a possible alternative to other solutions less radically opposed to one another: rather, it
constitutes a category of its own."[26] It is certainly not an
ideology—it is a way of living the gospel:

Nor is it [the Church's social doctrine] an
ideology, but rather the accurate formulation of the results of a careful reflection on
the complex realities of human existence,
in society and the international order, in
the light of faith and of the church's tradition. Its main aim is to interpret these realities, determining their conformity with or
divergence from the Gospel teaching on
man and his vocation, a vocation which is
at once earthly and transcendent; its aim is

thus to guide the Christian behavior. It therefore belongs to the field, not of ideology, but of theology, and particularly of moral theology.[27]

Reflection: The church's social teaching doctrine is the contemporary expression of the traditional Catholic image of the Mystical Body.

Saint Paul in his analogy for the unity of the Christian community uses the human body—when one member suffers, all parts of the body feel the pain. "If one member suffers, all the members suffer with it" (1 Cor 12:26). The Second Vatican Council, in its document on the church, *Lumen Gentium*, acknowledged the unity of the People of God, united throughout the world, "present among all nations on earth, since [it] takes its citizens from every race, citizens of a Kingdom that by its nature is not of this world but from heaven. In fact, all the faithful spread throughout the world are in communion with one another through the Holy Spirit . . ." (no. 13). This same Conciliar document describes the nature of the body of Christ in today's world: "In virtue of this catholicity, each individual part brings its gifts to the other parts and to the entire church, and thus the whole and individual parts are reinforced by communicating with each other, working together to attain fulfillment in unity" (no. 13).

We are called to appreciate and understand more fully our relationship to the other members of the Mystical Body, part of the mystery that is the church. "The Church, as the Mystical Body of Christ, penetrates and embraces us all. The spiritual, mystical dimensions of the church are much greater than any sociological statistics could ever possibly show."[28]

This perspective of the Mystical Body can help us in our perspective of the unity among all peoples. The social doctrine of the church provides us with an international outlook, guided by the insights of the Second Vatican Council and the recent encyclicals. John Paul II calls us to see the relationship we have with those who are not blessed with our Western material resources and privileges:

> Today, furthermore, given the worldwide dimension which the social question has consumed, this love of preference for the poor, and the decisions which it inspires in us, cannot but embrace the immense multitudes of the hungry, the needy, the homeless, those without medical care and, above all, those without hope of a better future. It is impossible not to take account of the existence of these realities. To ignore them would mean becoming like the "rich man" who pretended not to know the beggar Lazarus lying at the gate (cf. Lk 16:19–31).[29]

Reflection: Because we realize our dignity, rights, and responsibilities, in relationship with others, we need to continue to build a community that empowers people to attain their full human potential.

It has been said that a key test of a parish's "Catholicity" is its willingness to go beyond its boundaries to serve those in need and work for global justice and peace.[30] Should a social justice committee, for example, develop a program that could assist refugees or immigrants, or any others exposed to unjust discrimination, the community pierces the veil of ignorance and distrust that alienates and separates into stereotypes and misunderstanding. Many parishes make as a part of their Lenten programs "Operation Rice Bowl," a program of Catholic Relief Services which helps parishioners learn of the human needs around the world and offers them an opportunity to respond to those needs. In ways such as these—by working with others with common goals that breach religious, racial, ethnic and other lines—we can participate in the solidarity in action called for by Catholic social teaching. As John Paul II reminds us, such ministry reinforces basic Christian social doctrine teachings:

> It is necessary to state once more the characteristic principle of Christian social doctrine: the goods of this world are originally meant for all. . . . Likewise, in this concern for the poor, one, must not overlook that special form of poverty which consists in being deprived of fundamental human rights, in particular the right to religious freedom and also the right to freedom of economic initiative.[31]

Such local effort is participation in the Mystical Body of Christ and in a real way can actualize what is taught by the *Catechism of the Catholic Church* in regards to solidarity: "Socio-economic problems can be resolved only with the help of all the forms of solidarity: solidarity of the poor among themselves, between rich and poor, of workers among themselves, between employers and employees in a business, solidarity among nations and peoples. International solidarity is a requirement of the moral order; world peace depends in part upon this" (*C.C.C.*, no. 1941). Such steps, even if perceived by those who participate as small efforts given the size of the task, can still greatly impact the status quo. The catechism goes on to state: "In place of abusive . . . financial systems among nations, and the arms race, there must be substituted a common effort to mobilize resources toward objectives of moral, cultural and economic development, 'redefining the priorities and hierarchies of values'" (*C.C.C.*, no. 2438). Mother Teresa, in speaking about the good that can be done by small actions and their impact, once said: "Be faithful in small things because it is in them that your strength lies."[32] Whatever efforts we make, no matter how localized, or seemingly insignificant, to extend our solidarity towards those who are marginalized within our midst, impacts the greater society, for we are one body in the Lord.

> Almighty and ever-living God,
> empower your one human family to join
>   hands
> on our journey of faith.
> Send us your Spirit of hope,
> so that we may work
> to alleviate human suffering
> and foster charity and justice in our world
> Amen.

Reflection Questions:

1. What does it mean to be a "person of peace?"

2. Who do you look to as role models for lives marked by the approach of non-violence?

3. How do I become a person whose inner spirit and life are directed toward peace?

4. How can I best, in my own circumstances, reflect peace in my dealings with others?

5. What moral responsibility do I have to educate others in the ways of peace?

6. How do we advocate for solidarity among peoples in a time of terrorism?

Conclusion

As has been seen, Catholic social action and the work for justice is rooted in Scriptures and in our understanding of the value and dignity of the human person. Since each person is made in the image and likeness of God, redeemed by Jesus Christ, the Catholic church has continued to proclaim the sanctity and beauty of human life, from conception to natural death. Although the U.S. bishops have helpfully organized the teachings of social justice into seven broad categories or themes, the basis of each theme can be said to flow from this understanding: "Each person has inherent value and dignity, which comes from God and independent of any human accomplishment or quality."[1]

Our Hebrew and Christian Scriptures forcefully invite us to reflect on what should be a passion for justice, as articulated by the prophets and lived by Jesus Christ who came to bring glad tidings to the poor, liberty to captives and recovery of sight to the blind (see Lk 4:18–19).

The development of our Catholic social consciousness has also been formed by our theological reflection. Our knowledge of the Triune God has revealed the communitarian nature of our human relationships and our call to be social beings, concerned about our neighbor. Governments and social institutions have a duty and responsibility to integrate the participation of all people in the structures that shape public life. "A central moral test of political, legal and economic institutions is what they do *to* people, what they do *for* people, and how people might *participate* in them."[2]

The call to be Christ to the world and advocate for social justice cannot be extraneous from our spirituality or relationship with Christ. As the popes have articulated in various social justice encyclicals and as reinforced by our own bishops in their various pastoral letters, Catholic social teaching is not optional or fringe. It must be lived by the People of God who seek to build the kingdom of God. It is our vocation to move from our relationship with God "to live our faith in the world, and to apply the values of the Scriptures and the teaching of the church in our own families and parishes, in our work and service and in local communities, the nation and the world."[3] Gradually we learn as we pray, celebrate liturgy and read the Scriptures, that there is a social mission for each believer. "In seeking justice and peace, we witness to the reign of God in our midst. In prayer, we find the reasons, the strength, and the call to follow Jesus in the ways of charity, justice and peace."[4]

We are blessed to see many parishes, various faith communities and Christians attempting to live out the message of the social gospel, evangelizing by a fruitful proclamation of justice and solidarity, flowing from their knowledge and love for Jesus Christ. They have truly found their identity. "We cannot call ourselves Catholic unless we hear and heed the church's teaching to serve those in need, to protect human life and dignity, and to pursue justice and peace."[5]

Notes

Introduction

1. United States Catholic Conference, *Sharing Catholic Social Teaching: Challenges and Directions*, (Washington, D.C.: USCC, 1998), 1.
2. Thomas Merton, *Life and Holiness* (New York: Doubleday, 1963), 90.
3. John F. Kavanaugh, *(Still) Following Christ in a Consumer Society*, (Maryknoll, N.Y.: Orbis Books, 1991), 83.
4. Bernard Häring, *To Do Justice: A Christian Social Conscience* (Liguori, Mo: Liguori Publications, 1999), 5.
5. Ibid., 7.
6. Congregation for the Doctrine of the Faith, *Instruction on Christian Freedom and Liberation* (Washington, D.C.: U.S.C.C., 1986), 42.
7. Samuel Gregg, *Challenging the Modern World: Karol Wojtyla/John Paul II and the Development of Catholic Social Teaching* (New York: Lexington, 1999), 15.
8. Kavanaugh, 162.
9. Ibid., 165.

Chapter One

1. *Rochester Democrat and Chronicle*, June 25, 2002, p. 1.
2. John Paul II, *The Ecological Crisis: A Common Responsibility, Message of His Holiness Pope John Paul II for the Celebration of the World Day of Peace* (Washington, D.C.: U.S.C.C., 1990), 5, No. 4.
3. Ibid., No. 5.

4. Murray Bodo, *The Way of St. Francis: The Challenge of Franciscan Spirituality for Everyone* (New York: Image Books, 1985), 4.

5. Ibid., 7.

6. Lawrence Cunningham and Dennis Stock, *Saint Francis of Assisi,* (New York: Harper & Row, 1981), 58.

7. Ibid., 61.

8. *The Ecological Crisis*, 13, No. 16.

9. Cunningham and Stock, 62.

10. Ibid., 77.

11. Ibid., 80.

12. Bodo, 145.

13. Ibid., 143–144.

14. *The Ecological Crisis*, 14, No. 16.

15. Walter Brueggemann, *The Message of the Psalms: A Theological Commentary* (Minneapolis: Augsburg Publishing, 1984), 25.

16. C. S. Lewis, *Reflections on the Psalms* (New York: Harcourt, Brace & Company, 1958), 83.

17. Ibid.

18. Brueggemann, 30.

19. Ibid., 32.

20. Ibid., 34.

21. Ibid., 35.

22. Lewis, 132.

23. *The Ecological Crisis*, 3, No. 1.

24. Ibid.

25. Häring, 15.

26. United States Catholic Conference, *Let the Earth Bless the Lord, God's Creation and Our Responsibility: A Catholic Approach to the Environment,* (Washington, D.C.: U.S.C.C., 1996), 16.

27. *Sharing Catholic Social Teaching*, 6.

28. Ibid.

29. Barbara Kohnen, "The Flourishing of the Human Family—Protecting the Environment: The Sustainable Development Model" in *Let the Earth Bless the Lord*, 19.
30. *The Ecological Crisis*, 5, No. 5.
31. Ibid.
32. *Catechism of the Catholic Chruch*, No. 1147.
33. John L. McKenzie, *Dictionary of the Bible* (New York: Macmillan, 1965), 160.
34. *Crossing the Threshold of Hope*, 20.
35. Ibid., 21.
36. C.C.C., No. 2415.
37. Häring, 47.
38. C.C.C., No. 2432.
39. *The Ecological Crisis*, 7, No. 7.
40. Häring, 49.
41. C.C.C., No. 2403.
42. *The Ecological Crisis*, 9, No. 9.
43. "Prayers of Blessing and Praise for All Occasions", Hugo Schlesinger and Humberto Porto, in *Let the Earth Bless the Lord*, 15.

Chapter Two

1. Daniel J. Harrington, *The Gospel of Matthew* (Collegeville: Liturgical Press, 1991), 18.
2. William Barclay, *The Gospel of Matthew*, vol. 2, (Philadelphia: Westminster Press, 1958), 17.
3. Ibid.
4. Richard Rohr, *The Good News According to Luke* (New York: Crossroad, 1997), 145.
5. John C. L. Gibson, *Genesis*, vol. 1 (Philadelphia: Westminster Press, 1981), 70.
6. Ibid., 77.

7. *C.C.C.*, No. 264.

8. Avery R. Dulles, *The Splendor of Faith: The Theological Vision of Pope John Paul II* (New York: Herder and Herder, 1999), 147.

9. John Paul II, January 27, 1999, St. Louis, Missouri, in statement of the Administrative Board of the United States Conference of Catholic Bishops, "A Good Friday Appeal to End the Death Penalty" (Washington, D.C.: U. S. C. C. B., 1999) 1.

10. Michael Pennock, *Catholic Social Teaching: Learning and Living Justice* (Notre Dame: Ave Maria Press, 2000), 87.

11. Bishop Joseph Fiorenza, Statement of the U.S. Conference of Catholic Bishops' President on the Execution of Timothy McVeigh, (Washington, D.C.: U.S.C.C.B., 2001).

12. "Good Friday Appeal," 1

13. Ibid., 2.

14. Theodore Cardinal McCarrick, "101 Reasons to Abandon the Death Penalty" (Washington, D.C.: U.S.C.C.B., 2002.

15. John Paul II, *1999 Letter to the Elderly* (Washington D.C.: U.S.C.C.B., 1999), 5, No. 6.

16. Ibid., 6, No. 8.

17. Ibid., No. 9.

18. *C.C.C.*, No. 2278.

19. Ibid., No. 2279.

20. *Letter to the Elderly*, 7, No. 9.

21. Ibid., No. 10.

22. Ibid., No. 10.

23. *C.C.C.*, No. 2270.

24. Pennock, 90.

25. Dulles, 147.

26. United States Conference of Catholic Bishops, *Sharing Catholic Social Teaching, Challenges and*

Directions: Reflections of the U.S. Catholic Bishops (Washington, D.C.: U.S.C.C.B., 1998), 4.

27. Congregation for the Doctrine of the Faith, *Donum Vitae, The Gift of Life* (Washington, D.C.: U.S.C.C.B., 1987), III.

28. Catholic Bishops of the United States, "Living the Gospel of Life: A Challenge to American Catholics" (Washington, D.C.: U.S.C.C.B., 1998), 11, No. 32.

29. Ibid.

30. Ibid., No. 33.

31. Ibid., 12, No. 34.

32. Ibid., No. 35.

33. U.S. Bishops, "Welcome and Justice for Persons with Disabilities" (Washington, D.C.: U.S.C.C.B. 2002), 1, No. 3.

34. Campaign for Human Development, *Being Neighbor: The Catechism and Social Justice* (Washington, D.C.: U.S.C.C. 1998), 4.

Chapter Three

1. Rohr, 87.

2. Ibid.

3. John Paul II, *Crossing the Threshold of Hope*, ed. by Vittorio Messori (New York: Alfred A. Knopf, 1995), 37.

4. Ibid., 41.

5. Ibid.

6. C.C.C., No. 234.

7. C.C.C., No. 232.

8. Anthony J. Gittins, *A Presence That Disturbs: A Call to Radical Discipleship* (Liguori, Mo.: Liguori/Triumph, 2002), xi.

9. Ibid.

10. U.S. Catholic Bishops, "Follow the Way of Love: A Pastoral Message of the U.S. Catholic Bishops to Families On the Occasion of the United Nations 1994 International Year of the Family") Washington, D.C.: U.S.C.C.B.), 1994, 1.

11. Ibid., 2.

12. Ibid., 1.

13. *C.C.C.*, No. 2205.

14. "Follow the Way of Love," 4.

15. Ibid.

16. Ibid.

17. Ibid., 5.

18. Vatican Council II, *The Church in the Modern World*, tr. by Walter M. Abbott (New York: Guild Press, 1966), No. 25.

19. *C.C.C.*, No. 1879.

20. *The Church in the Modern World*, No. 25.

21. U.S. Bishops, *Everyday Christianity: To Hunger and Thirst for Justice* (Washington, D.C.: U.S.C.C.B.), 1998, 2.

22. *Everyday Christianity: To Hunger and Thirst for Justice*, 4.

23. Ibid.

24. Paul VI, *Encyclical Letter On the Development of Peoples, Populorum Progressio* (Boston: Daughters of St. Paul, 1967), 48, No. 81.

25. John Paul II, *The Gospel of Life, Evangelium Vitae* (Ottawa: Canadian Conference of Catholic Bishops, 1995), 164, No. 92

26. Ibid., 163, No. 92.

27. John Paul II, *Encyclical Letter On the Hundredth Anniversary of Rerum Novarum, Centesimus Annus* (Washington, D.C.: U.S.C.C., 1991), 67, No. 34.

28. Vatican Council II, *Dogmatic Constitution on the Church, Lumen Gentium*, No. 31.

29. William Droel, *Full Time Christians: The Real Challenge from Vatican II* (Mystic, Conn: Twenty-Third Publications, 2002), 7.
30. Ibid., 8.
31. Ibid., 71.
32. Droel, 71.
33. Catholic Campaign for Human Development, *Principles, Prophecy and Pastoral Response* (Washington, D.C.: U.S.C.C.B., 2001) 10.
34. *Being Neighbor*, 5.

Chapter Four

1. *Everyday Christianity: To Hunger and Thirst for Justice*, 1.
2. Ibid., 1–2.
3. Ibid., 2.
4. Droel, 7.
5. Ibid., 8.
6. Ibid.
7. Ibid.
8. Pope John XXIII, *Pacem in Terris, Peace on Earth* (Boston, Ma.: Daughters of St. Paul, 1963), 7, No. 2.
9. Ibid., 8, No. 3.
10. Ibid., 9, No. 9.
11. Ibid., 9, Nos. 9- 12.
12. *The Church in the Modern World*, No. 3.
13. Droel, 87.
14. Ibid.
15. *C.C.C.*, No. 1916.
16. Ibid.
17. *C.C.C.*, No. 1917.
18. Droel, 100.
19. Ibid.
20. Ibid., 101.

21. *C.C.C.*, No. 2237.
22. *Living the Gospel of Life*, 9, No. 24.
23. Ibid., No. 25.
24. Ibid.
25. *C.C.C.*, No. 2242.
26. *C.C.C.*, No. 2244.
27. *The Church in the Modern World*, No. 5.
28. *Living the Gospel of Life*, 9, No. 26.
29. John Paul II, *Sollicitudo Rei Socialis, For the Twentieth Anniversary of Populorum Progressio* (Vatican City: Libreria Editrice Vaticana, 1987), 22, No. 14.
30. Ibid.
31. Ibid., 23.
32. Ibid.
33. National Conference of Catholic Bishops, *Economic Justice for All: Pastoral Letter on Catholic Social Teaching and the U.S. Economy* (Washington, D.C.: U.S.C.C., 1986), xi, No. 18.
34. *Peace on Earth*, 16, No. 45.
35. Häring, 59.
36. *Economic Justice for All*, 121, No. 251.
37. Ibid.
38. Ibid., 122, No. 252.
39. Ibid., 123, No. 254.
40. Ibid.
41. Ibid.
42. Ibid., No. 257, 124.
43. *The Church in the Modern World*, No. 74. In addition, in regards to armed resistance to oppression by political authorities, the *Catechism of the Catholic Church* is quite clear in outlining conditions, all of which must be met, for *legitimacy*: 1) there is certain, grave and prolonged violation of fundamental rights; 2) all other means of redress have been exhausted; 3) such resistance will not provoke worse

disorders; 4) there is well-founded hope of success; and 5) it is impossible reasonably to foresee any better solution (No. 2243).

44. Häring, 59.
45. Ibid., 60.
46. *For the Twentieth Anniversary of Populorum Progressio, (Sollicitudo Rei Socialis)*, 75, No. 39.
47. United States Catholic Conference, *Novena for Justice and Peace* (Washington, D.C.: U.S.C.C., 1998), 8.

Chapter Five

1. Bruce J. Malina, *The Social World of Jesus and the Gospels* (New York: Routledge, 1996), 47.
2. Kavanaugh, 15.
3. John P. Meier, *A Marginal Jew: Rethinking the Historical Jesus*, vol. 1 (New York: Doubleday, 1991), 282.
4. Rohr, 136.
5. Ibid.
6. Ibid., 137.
7. *Principles, Prophecy and a Pastoral Response*, 17.
8. Kavanaugh, 21.
9. *Economic Justice for All*, vii, No. 6.
10. Kavanaugh, 29.
11. *Economic Justice for All*, 33, No. 64.
12. Ibid., 39, No. 77.
13. Ibid.
14. Ibid.
15. Ibid. 40, No. 78.
16. Ibid., ix, No. 13.
17. Ibid., xi, No. 16.
18. Gittins, *A Presence That Disturbs*, 116.
19. Ibid., 117.
20. Ibid., 157.

21. *Crossing the Threshold of Hope*, 128.
22. C.C.C., No. 2444.
23. *Everyday Christianity*, 1.
24. Ibid.
25. *Economic Justice for All*, 12, No. 24.
26. Ibid., 13, No. 27.
27. Ibid., 14.
28. William Barclay, *The Letters of James and Peter*, (Philadelphia: Westminster Press, 1977), 76.
29. *Economic Justice for All*, 50, No. 99.
30. Ibid., 51.
31. Ibid., 51-52, No. 100.
32. Ibid., 52.
33. John Paul II, *Centesimus Annus, On the Hundredth Anniversary of Rerum Novarum* (Washington, DC: U. S. C. C., 1991), 64, No. 33.
34. Ibid., 65.
35. Ibid., 66.
36. *Economic Justice for All*, 60, No. 120.
37. Ibid., 61, No. 123.
38. *Crossing the Threshold of Hope*, 26.
39. Kavanaugh, 159.
40. Ibid., 160.
41. Ibid.
42. Ibid., 163.
43. *Being Neighbor*, 7.

Chapter Six

1. Meier, 281.
2. Ibid.
3. Ibid.

4. Leo XIII, *Rerum Novarum, On the Condition of the Working Class* (Boston, Ma.: Daughters of St. Paul, 9, No. 11.

5. Ibid., 19, No. 31.

6. Ibid., No. 32.

7. Ibid., 48, No. 76.

8. Ibid., 34-35, No. 56.

9. Ibid., 52, No. 82.

10. John Paul II, *Laborem Exercens, On Human Work* (Ottawa: Canadian Conference of Catholic Bishops, 1981), 86, No. 25.

11. Ibid., 90, No. 26.

12. *Sharing Catholic Social Teaching*, 5.

13. George Weigel, *Witness to Hope: The Biography of John Paul II* (New York: Harper-Collins, 1999), 56.

14. John Paul II, *Gift and Mystery: On the Fiftieth Anniversary of My Priestly Ordination* (New York: Doubleday, 1996), 21-22.

15. Ibid., 21.

16. *The Church in the Modern World*, No. 34.

17. Ibid.

18. Roger Cardinal Mahony, "A Jubilee for Workers: Challenges and Opportunities for the New Millennium" (Washington, D.C.: U.S.C.C.B., 2000), 1.

19. Ibid.

20. Ibid.

21. Ibid., "The Dignity of Work and Workers: The Message of *Laborem Exercens*" (Washington, D.C.: U.S.C.C.B., 2001), 1.

22. Ibid.

23. Ibid., 2.

24. Ibid., "A Jubilee for Workers: Challenges and Opportunities for the New Millennium (Washington, D.C.: U.S.C.C.B., 2000), 2.

25. Ibid., "Social Security and Solidarity", Washington, DC: United States Conference of Catholic Bishops, Labor Day, September 6, 1999, 1.
26. Ibid., 2
27. "The Dignity of Work and Workers: The Message of *Laborem Exercens*", 2.
28. Edward T. Mechmann. *God, Society and the Human Person: The Basics of Catholic Social Teaching* (New York: Alba House, 2000), 50.
29. *Being Neighbor*, 8.

Chapter Seven

1. Tad Szulc, *Pope John Paul II: The Biography* (New York: Scribner, 1995), 343.
2. Pope John Paul II, *Sollicitudo Rei Socialis, For the Twentieth Anniversary of Populorum Progressio* (Vatican City: Libreria Editrice Vaticana, 1987) 75, No. 39.
3. Ibid.
4. Ibid.
5. Ibid.
6. Ibid.
7. Ibid., 76.
8. Ibid.
9. Ibid.
10. Ibid.
11. *Sharing Catholic Social Teaching*, 5.
12. United States Conference of Catholic Bishops, "A Pastoral Message: Living With Faith and Hope After September 11" (Washington, D.C.: U.S.C.C.B., November 14, 2001, 2.
13. Ibid.
14. Ibid.
15. Ibid.

16. Ibid.
17. John Paul II, "World Day of Peace Message" (Washington, D.C.: U.S.C.C.B., Dec. 8, 2001) 5, No. 12.
18. Ibid., *Crossing the Threshold of Hope*, 93.
19. Ibid., 94.
20. *World Day of Peace Message*, 6, No. 14.
21. *Peace on Earth*, 8, No. 7.
22. National Conference of Catholic Bishops, *The Challenge of Peace: God's Promise and Our Response* (Washington, D.C.: U.S.C.C., 1983), 73-74, No. 236.
23. *The Twentieth Anniversary of Populorum Progressio*, 81, No. 41.
24. Ibid., 81-82.
25. Ibid., 82.
26. Ibid., 83.
27. Ibid.
28. *Crossing the Threshold of Hope*, 143.
29. *On the Twentieth Anniversary of Populorum Progressio*, 85, No. 42.
30. National Conference of Catholic Bishops, *Communities of Salt and Light: Reflections on the Social Mission of the Parish* (Washington, D.C.: N.C.C.B., 1992), 12.
31. *On the Twentieth Anniversary of Populorum Progressio*, 86, No. 42.
32. José Luis González-Balado (ed.). *Heart of Joy: Mother Teresa* (Ann Arbor, Mich.: Servant Books, 1987), 83.

Conclusion

1. *Sharing Catholic Social Teaching*, 22.
2. Ibid., 24.
3. Ibid., 23.

4. National Conference of Catholic Bishops, *Communities of Salt and Life: Reflections on the Social Mission of the Parish* (Washington, D.C.: U.S.C.C.B., 1994), 5.

5. *Sharing Catholic Social Teaching*, 22.

Sources and Suggested Readings

Barclay, William. *The Gospel of Matthew*. Philadelphia: Westminster Press, 1958.

Bodo, Murray. *The Way of St. Francis: The Challenge of Franciscan Spirituality for Everyone*. New York: Image, 1985.

Brockman, James R. *Romero: A Life*. Maryknoll, N.Y.: Orbis Books, 1989.

Brueggemann, Walter. *The Message of the Psalms: A Theological Commentary*. Minneapolis: Augsburg, 1984.

Campaign for Human Development, United States Catholic Conference. *Being Neighbor: The Catechism and Social Justice*. Washington, D.C.: U.S.C.C., 1998.

———. *A Justice Prayer Book with Biblical Reflections*. Washington, D.C.: U.S.C.C., 1998

———. *Novena for Justice and Peace*. Washington, D.C.: U.S.C.C., 1998.

———. *Principles, Prophecy and a Pastoral Response: An Overview of Modern Catholic Social Teaching* (Revised Edition). Washington, D.C.: U.S.C.C.B., 2001.

———. *Scripture Guide*. Washington, D.C.: U.S.C.C., 1998

———. *Way of the Cross: Toward Justice and Peace*. Washington, D.C.: U.S.C.C., 1998.

Campaign for Human Development, United States Catholic Conference/Catholic Relief Services. *A Catholic Call to Justice: An Activity Book for Raising Awareness of Social Justice Issues*. Washington, D.C.: U.S.C.C., 1998.

Catechism of the Catholic Church. Mahwah, N.J.: Paulist Press, 1994.

Catholic Bishops of the United States. *Everyday Christianity: A Pastoral Reflection on Lay Discipleship for Justice in a New Millennium.* Washington, D.C.: U.S.C.C.B., 1999.

———— *Everyday Christianity: To Hunger and Thirst for Justice.* Washington, D.C.: U.S.C.C., 1998.

———— *Follow the Way of Love: A Pastoral Message of the U.S. Catholic Bishops to Families on the Occasion of the United Nations International Year of the Family.* Washington, D.C.: U.S.C.C.B., 1994.

———— Statement, *Living the Gospel of Life: A Challenge to American Catholics.* Washington, D.C.: U.S.C.C.B., 1998.

———— Statement, *Welcome and Justice for Persons with Disabilities: A Framework of Access and Inclusion.* Washington, D.C.: U.S.C.C.B., 2002.

Documents of Vatican Council II. Ed. by Walter M. Abbott. New York: Guild Press, 1966.

Devananda, Angelo. *Mother Teresa: Contemplative in the Heart of the World.* Ann Arbor, Mich.: Servant books, 1985.

Droel, William. *Full Time Christians: The Real Challenge from Vatican II.* Mystic, Conn.: Twenty-Third Publications, 2002.

Duffy, Regis A. and Angelus Gambatese, eds. *Made in God's Image: The Catholic Vision of Human Dignity.* New York: Paulist Press, 1999.

Dulles, Avery. *The Splendor of Faith: The Theological Vision of Pope John Paul II.* New York: Crossroad, 1999.

Fiorenza, Joseph. *Statement of the President of the U.S. Conference of Catholic Bishops on the Execution of Timothy McVeigh.* Washington, D.C.: U.S.C.C.B., 2001.

Gibson, John C. L. *Genesis, V. 1.* Philadelphia: Westminster Press, 1981.

Gittins, Anthony J. *A Presence that Disturbs: A Call to Radical Discipleship*. Liguori, Mo.: Liguori/Triumph, 2002.

González-Balado, José Luis. *Stories of Mother Teresa: Her Smile and Her Words*. Liguori, Mo.: Liguori Publications, 1983.

———— *Heart of Joy: The Transforming Power of Self Giving, Mother Teresa*. Ann Arbor, Mich.: Servant Books, 1987.

Gregg, Samuel. *Challenging the Modern World: Karol Wojtyla/John Paul II and the Development of Catholic Social Teaching*. New York: Lexington, 1999.

Häring, Bernard. *To Do Justice: A Christian social Conscience*. Liguori, Mo.: Liguori, 1999.

Harrington, Daniel J. *The Gospel of Matthew*. Collegeville: Liturgical Press, 1991.

John XXIII. *Encyclical Letter, Peace on Earth* (Pacem in Terris). Boston: Daughters of St. Paul, 1963.

John Paul II. *Crossing the Threshold of Hope*. Ed. by V. Messori. New York: Alfred A. Knopf, 1995.

———— *The Ecological Crisis: A Common Responsibility, Message of His Holiness Pope John Paul II for the Celebration of the World Day Of Peace*. Washington, D.C.: U.S.C.C., 1990.

———— *Encyclical letter on the Gospel of Life (Evangelium Vitae)*. Ottawa, Canada: Canadian Conference of Catholic Bishops, 1995.

———— *Encyclical Letter On Human Work (Laborem Exercens)*. Ottawa, Canada: Canadian Conference of Bishops, 1981.

———— *Encyclical Letter on the Hundredth Anniversary of Rerum Novarum (Centesimus Annus)*. Washington, D.C.: U.S.C.C., 1991.

——— *Encyclical Letter on the Social Concern of the Church (Sollicitudo Rei Socialis)*. Vatican City: Libreria Editrice Vaticana, 1987.

——— *Gift and Mystery: On the Fiftieth Anniversary of My Priestly Ordination*. New York: Doubleday, 1996.

——— *Letter to the Elderly*. Washington, D.C.: U.S.C.C.B., 1999.

——— *World Day of Peace Message*. Washington, D.C.: U.S.C.C.B., 2001.

Kavanaugh, John F. *Following Christ in a Consumer Society* (Revised Edition). Maryknoll, N.Y.: Orbis Books, 1991.

Leo XIII. *Encyclical Letter On the Condition of the Working Class (Rerum Novarum)*. Boston: Daughters of St. Paul, 1891.

Lewis, C. S. *Reflections on the Psalms*. New York: Harcourt, Brace & Co., 1958.

Mahony, Roger. *Labor Day Statement, A Jubilee for Workers: Challenges and Opportunities for the New Millennium*. Washington, D.C.: U.S.C.C.B., 2000.

——— *Labor Day Statement, The Message of Laborem Exercens*. Washington, D.C.: U.S.C.C.B., 2001.

——— *Labor Day Statement, Social Security and Solidarity*. Washington, D.C.: U.S.C.C.B., 1999.

Malina, Bruce J. *The Social World of Jesus and the Gospels*. New York: Routledge, 1996.

McCarrick, Theodore. Statement, *101 Reasons to Abandon the Death Penalty*. Washington, D.C.: U.S.C.C.B., 2002.

McKenna, Kevin E. *A Concise Guide to Catholic Social Teaching*. Notre Dame: Ave Maria Press, 2002.

McKenzie, John L. *Dictionary of the Bible*. New York: Macmillan, 1965.

Mechmann, Edward T. *God, Society and the Human Person: The Basics of Catholic Social Teaching.* New York: Alba House, 2000.

Meier, John P. *A Marginal Jew: Rethinking the Historical Jesus, Vol. 1.* New York: Doubleday, 1991.

Merton, Thomas. *Life and Holiness.* New York: Image Books, 1963.

National Conference of Catholic Bishops. *Communities of Salt and Light: Reflections on the Social Mission of the Parish.* Washington, D.C.: U.S.C.C., 1994

———— *The Challenge of Peace: God's Promise and Our Response.* Washington, D.C.: USCC., 1983.

———— *Economic Justice for All: Pastoral Letter on Catholic Social Teaching and the U.S. Economy.* Washington, D.C.: U.S.C.C., 1986.

Paul VI. *Encyclical Letter On The Development of Peoples (Populorum Progressio).* Boston: Daughters of St. Paul, 1967.

Pennock, Michael. *Catholic Social Teaching: Learning and Living Justice.* Notre Dame: Ave Maria Press, 2000.

Rohr, Richard. *The Good News According to Luke: Spiritual Reflections.* New York: Crossroad, 1997.

Romero, Oscar, compiled and translated by James R. Brockman. *The Violence of Love.* Farmington, Pa.: Plough Publishing, 1998.

Szulc, Tad. *Pope John Paul II: The Biography.* New York: Scribner, 1995.

United States Catholic Conference. *Let the Earth Bless the Lord: God's Creation and Our Responsibility, A Catholic Approach to the Environment.* Washington, D.C.: U.S.C.C., 1996.

———— *Sharing Catholic Social Teaching, Challenges and Directions: Reflections of the U.S. Catholic Bishops.* Washington, D.C.: U.S.C.C., 1998.

United States Conference of Catholic Bishops,
      Administrative Board. "A Good Friday Appeal to
      End the Death Penalty." Washington, DC:
      U.S.C.C.B., 1999.
—————— *A Pastoral Message: Living With Faith and Hope
      After September 11*. Washington, D.C.: U.S.C.C.B.,
      2001.
Weigel, George. *Soul of the World: Notes on the Future of
      Public Catholicism*. Grand Rapids: William B.
      Eerdmans, 1996.
—————— *Witness to Hope: The Biography of John Paul II*.
      New York: Harper-Collins, 1999.

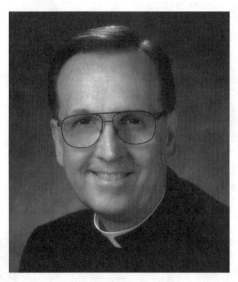

Rev. Kevin E. McKenna is a past president of the Canon Law Society of America and serves as pastor at St. Cecilia Parish in Rochester, New York. Ordained in 1977, Fr. McKenna received his doctorate degree in canon law from St. Paul University in Ottawa in 1990. He is the author of numerous articles and three previous books, *The Ministry of Law in the Church Today, A Concise Guide to Canon Law,* and *A Concise Guide to Catholic Social Teaching.*